SCHOOL ORGANIZATION
FOR THE
MENTALLY RETARDED

SCHOOL ORGANIZATION FOR THE MENTALLY RETARDED

BASIC GUIDES

Second Edition

By

STANLEY E. JACKSON, Ed.D.

Special Assistant to the Executive Director
The Council for Exceptional Children
Arlington, Virginia

and

GEORGE R. TAYLOR, Ph.D.

Director of Special Education
Coppin State College
Baltimore, Maryland

CHARLES C THOMAS • PUBLISHER
Springfield • Illinois • U.S.A.

Published and Distributed Throughout the World by

CHARLES C THOMAS • PUBLISHER

Bannerstone House

301-327 East Lawrence Avenue, Springfield, Illinois, U.S.A.

© *1973, by* CHARLES C THOMAS • PUBLISHER

ISBN 0-398-02742-0

Library of Congress Catalog Card Number: 72-93215

Printed in the United States of America

R-1

CONTENTS

SCHOOL ORGANIZATION
FOR THE
MENTALLY RETARDED

CHAPTER 1

INTRODUCTION

I T is generally accepted today by our society that all children are entitled to equality of educational opportunity. There is recognition of the fact that the perpetuation and improvement of the democratic way of life depends upon an educated citizenry. Millions of dollars are spent on public education so that all the children of all the people may have the opportunity for learning how to live happily, cooperatively, and successfully in a democratic society.

For many children, unfortunately, public school attendance does not guarantee equality of educational opportunity. This is evident when a look is taken at school records of pupil failure, maladjustment, and withdrawal. This is equally evident when young school graduates are unable to meet the demands and responsibilities of citizenship and become liabilities of the community. While the school does not and should not assume full responsibility for these failures, it shares responsibility with the community when it does not do its best to help each individual become the best person possible. A major function of the public school is to recognize each pupil as a unique personality and to help each one develop his abilities to the fullest in a socially acceptable and desirable way. The educational program must, therefore, take carefully into account the individual differences among pupils; all should not be expected to have the same purposes, to progress at similar rates, or to achieve identical ends. This is especially true of those pupils who deviate markedly in some respect from children in general.

Children who do deviate greatly and for whom a differentiated school curriculum is needed are commonly called exceptional children. They are generally grouped on the basis of their major deviation or handicap and may be classified as follows: (1) the physically handicapped, (2) the mentally handicapped, (3) the intellectually gifted, (4) the emotionally unstable, (5) those with special health impairments, (6) the blind and partially sighted, (7) the deaf and hard of hearing, (8) speech defectives, (9) the socially maladjusted, and (10) the multiple handicapped. These exceptional pupils often make up a high percentage of the school's failures. This is particularly true when the school is organized and administered in such a manner that it cannot adequately provide for their various differences.

Among exceptional children, the mentally retarded* constitute a sizeable group that requires a generous share of most educators' time, thought, and action. The public school thus faces a special challenge in providing suitable education for these children who deviate decidedly, in their subnormal mental development, from most children. The school usually attempts to provide adequately for these exceptional children, but its efforts are often far from successful for most of them. In order to provide a realistic program for retardates, administrators should select appropriate goals or objectives, program and sequence instructional tasks, insist upon well-trained personnel, provide appropriate supportive services, and seek community and parental support, based upon the needs, interests, and abilities of the children. Each pupil, regardless of his intellectual status, is entitled to an education that will enable him to achieve maximum growth and development in socially desirable directions.

During the early centuries of Western history the mentally retarded received vacillating, unscientific treatment that ranged from persecution to reverence. The ancient Greeks left retarded infants to die on the mountainside or cast them into rivers, with the approval of society. Romans retained retardates as servants or to afford amusement. Europeans, generally, were superstitious and regarded retardates as devils or having the power to generate evil. Prior to the nineteenth century these beliefs were well intrenched in Western cultures. Consequently, it was a common practice to consider retarded individuals less than human.

---

*Mental retardation refers to (1) subaverage general intellectual functioning, (2) which originates during the developmental period, and is associated with impairments in adaptive behavior. (See Chapter 2 for further discussion and references.)

A more enlightened viewpoint arose during the latter part of the nineteenth century as there began the scientific study and education of persons with limited mental endowment. From the ranks of the pioneers in this movement emerged such noted physician-teachers as the French doctors, Jean Itard (1775-1838) and Edward Sequin (1812-1880), and Marie Montessori (1869-1952) of Italy. These pioneers demonstrated the educability of the mentally handicapped through the use of methods that emphasized sensorimotor experiences. Later, the outstanding work of Alfred Binet (1857-1911) in France directed attention to the problems of measuring intelligence and identifying "mentally backward children." The Binet-Simon general intelligence test, which was an outgrowth of Binet's exploratory work, was standardized for American children by Lewis M. Terman in 1916 and opened the era of mental testing in the United States.

Improved testing procedures and compulsory school attendance laws brought increasing numbers of children with subnormal intelligence to the attention of the public school authorities. This heightened the problem of providing adequate education for these so-called "laggards" who did not belong in institutions, yet could not advance through school at the expected rate. In 1896, Providence, Rhode Island, established the first public school class for "backward children." During the next half century, school systems throughout the nation followed the lead of Providence and formed special classes for the mentally handicapped mature enough to be enrolled in public school. Concurrently, numerous individuals such as Fernald Johnstone and Helinn Devereaux, of the Vineland Training School demonstrated that the mentally retarded could not become normal but many of them could be helped to lead happy and productive lives. Other leaders as Horace Mann, Samuel Howe, and Dorothea Dix, gave impetus to the movement of establishing residential schools. These new techniques had the common base of adapting the instruction to the ability of the child and of emphasizing the concrete aspects of experience rather than the abstract. It was proved that appropriate teaching procedures could be successful in helping subnormal individuals become competent citizens.

In our nation, efforts are continuous today to help the mentally retarded achieve their rightful dignity and worth. Currently, all states now have varying amounts of special school provisions for the mentally handicapped under various types of permissive or mandatory laws or regulations. It was reported in the Journal of the American Association on Mental Deficiency* that states provide services to the retarded and their parents either directly or through financial assistance to communities for the development of local services; and school programs for mildly retarded or educable children have made phenomenal growth in the last decade.

The public schools are not alone in providing assistance to the mentally handicapped. The post-1958 era signaled a period of significant fiscal breakthrough for the backing of various programs dealing with education for the retarded. Public Law 85-926, since amended, was enacted by Congress in 1958 and provided support for training professional personnel to work with the retarded. The law was subsequently amended to include support for training professional personnel in other areas of exceptionality, and by 1968 nearly 44,000 teachers, supervisors, specialists, and college instructors had been trained under this act. In fiscal year 1970, nearly 30 million dollars was requested from Congress to support this program. The federal government has manifested intense interest in solving problems resulting from mental retardation. Money has been appropriated to begin programs of prevention, identification, treatment, education, and rehabilitation. In addition, funds have been made available for the construction of facilities and for the administration of clinical and educational units for the mentally retarded.†

The development of parent and teacher groups and organizations interested in the education of the mentally retarded is indicative of rising community interests and responsibility. These groups have provided financial resources, community and national support, stimulated research, disseminated information, en-

---

*W. I. Gardner and H. W. Nisonger, "A Manual on Program Development in Mental Retardation," Monograph Supplement to the *American Journal of Mental Deficiency, 66*(4), (January, 1962), p. 308.
†Robert M. Smith, *An Introduction to Mental Retardation,* (New York, McGraw-Hill Book Company, 1971), pp. 33-36.

couraged passage of legislation in the support of exceptional children on local, state, and federal levels, and have insisted upon and obtained higher standards for institutions and personnel. Without the support of these groups it is generally agreed that the proliferation of programs for retardates would not be advanced as we know them today.

Public schools have been assisted also by a steady output of professional books and articles, disseminating the current findings and the varied problems in the field of mental retardation. Modern medical and psychological research continues to extend and improve knowledge and methods concerning the treatment, behavior and adjustment of mentally retarded children. These advances made through research have aided administrators in developing a better understanding of the behavior and biological correlates of mental retardation, especially showing that appropriate adaptive behavior can be shaped. Today, much of the pessimism concerning educating retarded children is gradually dissipating. It is generally accepted that a high percentage of mentally retarded children are capable of becoming useful, reliable citizens and that all who can profit from education are entitled to equal educational opportunities.

Mental retardates are of major concern to educators today because of the growing demands made upon subnormal individuals by the urgencies and complexities of modern life. Mental retardates become a large and costly problem to society when they are unable to meet social and economic responsibilities. Thus, each child should be guided in reaching his optimum growth, and able to plan and manage his own life, within the limits of his abilities. Conversely, educational opportunities should not be denied to any child, because he lacks the ability for making a contribution to society.

Teachers are the ones most directly concerned with the education of the mentally retarded, but their effectiveness depends in large measure upon the influence of administrators. The school environment which administrators help create can encourage or discourage, release or stifle, the development of ideas, the adoption of innovations, and the promotion of cooperative working arrangements for good education. It is a fact that administrators can facilitate or retard the degree of success of the school in meeting the needs of mentally retarded pupils.

Administrators thus have a major responsibility for providing the conditions and services that will contribute to effective education of the mentally retarded. Pupil grouping and placement, promotion, management of supplies and equipment, the testing program, and selection and assignment of teachers are among the aspects of school organization and administration which affect the education of all children.

How effectively these services contribute to the education of mentally subnormal pupils will determine the degree to which equal educational opportunities are provided for them. A first step would be to define objectives in light of the needs, abilities and interests of the children, and to sequenced tasks that will lead to desired behavior. Equally important will be activities and materials matched with the objectives of the program. By employing specificity and objectivity in instruction for retardates, administrators will better insure equal education opportunities for them. Administrators should insist upon well-defined objectives that are observable and measurable, as well as activities and materials sequenced in line with the stated objectives.

The lack of needed modifications in school organization and unsuitable administration of the educational program for the mentally retarded can result in undesirable consequences. Many mentally retarded children may experience several years of failure before being identified and receiving special service. It may also happen that these children will be placed with teachers who are unprepared to understand their problems and to select the influences which will best advance their growth.

The values and attitudes of teachers and their effects on pupil's self-perceptions and performances cannot be minimized. Discovering the pupil characteristics which a given teacher will accept or reject becomes a critical administrative question.* The competencies of teachers and administrators are more than a collection of objectives or instructional skills. They should consist of deep-seated philosophies underlying our democratic value of

*Peter Valletutti, "Integration vs Segregation: A Useless Dialectic," *The Journal of Special Education, 3*(4), (Winter, 1969), pp. 406-407.

education for all children, which rejects the misconception that education for certain segments of retarded children is unproductive.

CHAPTER 2

WHO ARE THE MENTALLY RETARDED?

MENTAL retardation is a relatively new descriptional term for the men, women, and children who have once been called feebleminded, mentally subnormal, mentally defective, backward, idiotic, imbecile, or moronic. Although this term is more acceptable than its predecessors with their heritage of stigma and ridicule, it is far from precise and has many interpretations and definitions. Generally, however, all authorities agree that mental retardation is the inability to learn and mature socially at the usual rate because of something that happened before birth, during birth, or in the developmental period up to the age of sixteen.

The mentally retarded range from the small minority so badly damaged mentally and as a rule, physically, that they need lifelong round the clock care, to the great majority who often look normal and with some supervision can hold jobs. In between, are a group who cannot ever get far academically or live without continual supervision, but who can be trained in self-help, self-care, and the performance of some elementary task. These groups shade into one another without clear lines of demarcation, but for practical purposes of education and care they are classified as: (1) educable: this group is composed of individuals who might be able to achieve some degree of independence and become self-supporting citizens, if proper instruction is provided, (2) trainable: those children who will not be able to achieve a level of independence as educable; instruction should be based upon the functional ability of the child; generally instruction should be geared toward self-care, social and emotional adjustment. This group of children usually will require constant supervision throughout their lives, and (3) profoundly: this group of children will very seldom reach self-support or be able to profit significantly from skills taught to trainable children. They will require permanent custodial care and support.

Various definitions are used in identifying the mentally retarded by various disciplines; which might denote a different meaning to the individual specialist. This lack of consensus can perhaps be attributed to various classifications or criteria employed. To alleviate much of the confusion concerning classifications, most authorities have accepted the definition proposed by the American Association on Mental Deficiency.

The following definition was offered by Heber:* "Mental retardation refers to subaverage, general intellectual functioning (individuals whose performance on suitable objective tests of general intellectual ability is one standard deviation below the general population mean on a standard intelligence test); which originates during the developmental period and is associated with impairment in adaptive behavior. Adaptive behavior is manifested in three principal ways: (1) maturation, (2) learning, and (3) social adjustment." The definition was subsequently revised in 1961: "Mental retardation refers to subaverage general intellectual functioning which originates during the developmental period and is associated with impairment in adaptive behavior." According to this definition the following terms stated that (1) subaverage refers to performance which is at least one standard deviation below the population mean of the age group involved on measures of general intellectual functioning, (2) the level of general intellectual functioning may be assessed by performance on one or more of the various objective tests which have been developed for that purpose and, (3) though the upper age limit of the development period cannot be precisely specified, it may be regarded for practical purposes as being approximately sixteen years.

The definition further specifies that the subaverage intellectual functioning must be reflected by impairment in adaptive behavior. Adaptive behavior refers primarily to the effectiveness of the individual in adapting to the natural and social demands of his environment. Impaired adaptive behavior may be reflected in:

1. Maturation: The rate of sequential development of self-help

*Rick Heber, "A Manual on Terminology and Classification in Mental Retardation," *Monograph Supplement to American Journal of Mental Deficiency,* 2nd Ed., 1961, p. 3.

skills of infancy and early childhood such as sitting, crawling, standing, and other behaviors.

2. Learning: The facility with which knowledge is acquired as a function of experience.

3. Social adjustment: During the preschool and school years this is reflected, in large measure, in the level and manner in which the child relates to parents, other adults, and to his peers.*

The definition proposed by the AAMD has been the subject of much debate in recent years; nevertheless, a large majority of professional personnel have accepted this definition. Currently the Committee on Terminology and Classification is considering a review of the present classification system, partly due to a large percentage of children who are labeled retarded because they fall one standard deviation below the mean. Many professionals argued that children labeled as culturally deprived, according to this definition, would be classified as retarded because they usually fall one standard deviation below the mean on a standardized test.

In terms of educational potential, retarded children are described as (1) the educable mentally retarded: those with intelligence quotients from 50 to 75, (2) trainable mentally retarded: those with intelligence quotients from 25 to 50, and (3) profoundly retarded: with intelligence quotients below 25.

Educable retarded children are capable of being educated within limits and may achieve an academic competence of fourth or fifth grade level. They are able to maintain a moderate amount of social adjustment and a satisfactory degree of self-support in occupations not requiring too much abstract thought. As adults, if properly trained, they can work in competitive employment, able to live independent lives and maintain a home and family.

Trainable children may attain an acceptable level of self-care, social adjustment to home and neighborhood, and a degree of economic usefulness via the home, residential facility, or sheltered workshop. They can profit from a program geared lower than that of educable. Generally, they have more physical defects than educable or normal children.

Total dependent children require assistance in personal care,

---

Ibid.

make little response to their environment, and usually require permanent institutionalization. As a group they have their share of motor, speech, language, and physical defects which far exceeds that of other groups of retarded children. Recently, proposals have been made to extend public school education down to these children. Some authorities argue that there is no economic justification for giving public school education to this group of children, since they will not be able to make significant contributions to society. Recent legal decisions requiring the education of all mentally handicapped children makes the issue an unsettled one. In the future, public schools may be required to provide education for all retarded children, including the profoundly retarded.

CHAPTER 3

WHAT IS THE SCHOOL'S RESPONSIBILITY TOWARD RETARDED CHILDREN?

CHILDREN who do deviate greatly and for whom a differentiated school curriculum is needed are commonly called exceptional children. Among exceptional children, the mentally retarded constitute a sizeable group that requires a generous share of most educators time, thought, and action. The public school thus faces a special challenge in providing a suitable education for these children who deviate decidedly, in their subnormal mental development. The school usually attempts to provide adequately for these exceptional children, but its efforts are often far from successful for most of them. Nevertheless, the school's responsibility still remains to provide equal educational opportunities for mentally retarded pupils who now fail to receive them. Providing equal educational opportunities for retarded children is intricate, expensive, and complex. The school must learn to draw upon the services of community agencies and groups to meet the many needs of the retarded. Coordinating community services will assist the mentally retarded individual in achieving his maximum growth and development in socially desirable directions. Pressure from various sources is demanding that the schools provide quality education for all exceptional children, especially the mentally retarded.

Interest in special education is increasing greatly, because of the events of recent years. The influence of parent movement groups is showing that they have a deep concern for the future and the welfare of retarded children. Social changes in attitude toward mentally retarded children is a significant factor that the parents have instilled into the minds of the general public. Federal, local, and state governments are financially supporting programs for retarded children through various agencies. With the establishment of health clinics in particular, the services rendered to the mentally retarded children are improving considerably. Mental health agencies and the schools are seeking new ways to help retarded children who were once excluded from school. These interests have lead to increased research in the fields of biochemistry, medicine, psychology, sociology, education, and other allied disciplines. This surge of interest has increased greatly our understanding of retarded children.

Due chiefly to these trends, educational opportunities are available to more retarded children in more parts of our country and in greater variety than ever before, despite a large gap between the number of those in need and those being serviced. Mackie* pointed out that the challenge of providing educational opportunities to the mentally retarded is being met by local, public and private schools, and by public and private residential schools. However, she indicated that most retarded children are being educated in public day school programs.

Since most retarded children are educated in public schools, it appears that the schools must assume the direct responsibility for improving educational provisions for retardates and provide an environment that is conducive for learning.

ADMINISTRATIVE RESPONSIBILITIES

As stated, teachers are the ones most directly concerned with the education of the mentally retarded, but their effectiveness depends in large measure upon the influence of administrators. The school environment which administrators help create can encourage or discourage, release or stifle, the development of ideas, the adoption of innovation, and the promotion of cooperative working arrangement for good education. It is a fact that administrators can facilitate or retard the degree of success of

*Romaine P. Mackie, *Special Education in the United States: Statistics 1948-1966.* New York, Teachers College Press, 1969.

the school in meeting the needs of retarded pupils. It is of prime importance that teachers have the support and guidance of able administrators. A modern program of supervision based on sound educational principles enables teachers to gain deeper understanding of the factors and principles underlying and influencing their practices. The effects of supervision by competent, adequately prepared administrators will be an improvement of the total teaching-learning process for retarded children.

Administrators thus have a major responsibility for providing the conditions and services that will contribute to effective education of the mentally retarded. Pupil grouping and placement, promotion, management of supplies and equipment, the testing program, and selection and assignment of teachers are among the aspects of school organization and administration which affect the education of all children. How effectively these services contribute to the education of mentally retarded pupils will determine the degree to which equal educational opportunities are provided for them.

GOALS OF SPECIAL EDUCATION

The goals of special education are similar to those of the education for all children. Their aims are to develop and utilize one's physical and mental aptitudes in a socially desirable way. Special education is committed to educating exceptional children by seeing that each child contributes to his own maintenance and becomes a personally and socially adequate person to the extent of his abilities.

The goals listed by the Education Policies Commission, for all children, are appropriate for the mentally retarded as well. These goals are self-realization, human relationships, economic efficiency, and civic responsibility.* Charney† categorized certain skills under the four goals for retarded children. Under self-realization goals are health habits, skills of everyday living, i.e.,

---

*Education Policies Commission. *Policies for Education in American Democracy.* (National Education Association, Washington, D. C., 1946), p. 189.
†Leo Charney and Edward Crosse. *The Teacher of the Mentally Retarded.* (New York, John Day Co., 1965), p. 62-66.

dressing, feeding, personal cleanliness, language development, perceptual training, safety, independent travel, and simple number and reading concepts based upon the children's abilities; under goals of human relationships are communication skills, manners, and group activities; economic efficiency includes simple tasks of following directions through performing simple chores and pre-vocational participation to working in a sheltered workshop or in the community; civic responsibility includes the rights, duties, and privileges enjoyed as a member of the community. (*See* Appendix A, pp. 117-128)

The fundamental purposes of special education are the same as those of regular education: the optimal development of the individual as a skillful, free, and purposeful person, able to plan and manage his own life and to reach his highest potential as an individual and as a member of society. Indeed, special education developed as a set of highly specialized areas of education in order to provide exceptional children with the same opportunities as other children for a meaningful, purposeful, and fulfilling life.

Perhaps the most important concept that has been developed in special education as the result of experiences with exceptional children, is that of the fundamental individualism of every child. The aspiration of special educators is to see every child as a unique composite of potentials, abilities, and learning needs for whom an educational program must be designed to meet his particular needs. From its beginnings, special education has championed the cause of children with learning problems. As professionals, special educators are dedicated to the optimal education of exceptional children and they reject the misconception of schooling that is nothing but custodial care.*

Special education for the retarded is now generally recognized as a service to those who cannot adapt to the traditional educational system. Special education appears to be the best vehicle to serve the needs of retarded children whose needs cannot be adequately met in the regular classroom. Therefore, special education should not be conceived as a separate entity within the school structure, but as an integral part of the total educational

*Policy statement: Call for Response, "Basic Commitments and Responsibilities to Exceptional Children," *Exceptional Children, 38*(2), (October, 1971), p. 182.

process, whereby children may receive services in various educational settings within the public school. Special instruction and methods for retarded children require that provisions must be made for their unique needs, and that school personnel be able to monitor, and instruct in a personalized manner.

EDUCATIONAL PROVISIONS

The public schools have an obligation to admit retarded children and to give them an opportunity to profit from school attendance. It is also the responsibility of the public schools to make provisions for children who can not benefit sufficiently from the instruction provided in the regular class. A centrally coordinated approach is needed to improve the educational program for retardates. Special education as now constituted can hardly be expected to handle adquately all of the needs of retarded children. Many school districts do not have adequate services for comprehensive psychological, social, medical and educational evaluation of retarded pupils; conversely, techniques used for educational diagnosis and evaluation are frequently inadequate.

LEGAL PRINCIPLES

Recently, public schools have increasingly assumed responsibility for educating most retarded children in our society. This surge of interest can not be significantly equated with the basic principle of free education for all children. The courts and mandates from local, state, and federal governments, have insisted that all children in our society have a right to free public education. The result has been the enactment of laws in most states to provide educational opportunities for retarded children of all ages. Unfortunately, the school's commitment to educational opportunities for retarded children has not caught up with the courts. Many retarded children are exempted from school solely on the grounds of their retardation, characteristics, or disruptive behavior. Unless the school has examined various approaches and techniques for meeting the needs of retarded children who have been excluded from school, there is the danger that the child's civil rights, as guaranteed by the courts, might be denied or abridged. Concomitantly, many school districts have been sued, charging that they have not provided educational opportunities for retarded children. In the event that retarded children must be excused or excluded from school, or in the event that they constitute a danger to themselves or their peers, for illness or medical treatment, they should be readmitted as soon as the reason for their exclusion has been determined or treated. Exclusion should be temporary, and as carefully as possible, outline specific procedures governing the child's re-entry to school. Administrators should examine the issue of suspension and exclusion carefully before recommending a plan. All possible techniques and resources should be carefully delineated before a decision is made. If at all possible, modification should be made in the program to keep the child in school by providing supportive and specialized services.

GUIDANCE

The purpose of guidance is to help the individual achieve personal and social adjustment through a better understanding and use of his abilities. Guidance, to be effective, is a continuous process that starts when the child first enters school, and should be available for as long a period of time as necessary. The administrator, the social worker, and teaching personnel should play formal or informal parts in the philosophy of continuous guidance; all will be important to the total concept. Although a special education program in essence is a guidance program, it should emphasize that one of the basic techniques of special education is personal guidance or individualization of instruction. Personal guidance can be equated with the recognition of the unique problems of each individual and the formulation of techniques for assisting the retarded child in solving his problems.

Vocational or occupational guidance is very important for the mentally retarded. School personnel responsible for training programs should consider and plan for the ultimate goal of placement for the retarded. They should be aware of the reported causes of vocational failures and should design programs to emphasize desirable behavior patterns. Through accurate appraisal of the retardates' vocational potential, suitable training programs, selective placement and improved understanding of the relevant factors in the community, the available benefits of training and placement program can be maximized.*

The guidance techniques used in special education should be similar to those employed in the regular school program, with some adjustment made to meet the special needs of the retarded and his family. School personnel should realize that the difficulties of guidance for the retarded may be intensified due to the many problems inherited with retardation. Nevertheless, guidance and counseling for the retarded should be designed to aid the child's adjustment to school from the time of his entrance through secondary and post school adjustment. Guidance activities should begin with initial contacts to acquaint parents and community with the school's educational program and be extended directly to the child as his needs dictate. Guidance services should also seek to provide school personnel with important data useful in planning and adjusting the school program to each child's needs.

GROUPING

Smith† wrote that using achievement level as the sole criterion for grouping retarded children is insufficient. The following point was advanced to support the above statement, two or more children achieving at the same level, having the same chronological age and intellectual ability, could be experiencing difficulty in a certain area, such as reading, for reasons which are completely different. Grouping for instruction requires that the teacher demonstrate clinical awareness of each child's pattern of strengths and weaknesses by frequently surveying the performance of students on important dimensions. Since many retarded children employ techniques of learning, irrespective of the one preferred by teachers, the teacher should know of these patterns and group

---

*Julius Cohen, "Employer Attitudes Toward Hiring Mentally Retarded Individuals," *American Journal of Mental Deficiency, 67*, (March, 1963), pp. 705-713.

†Robert M. Smith, *Clinical Teaching: Methods of Instruction for the Retarded,* (New York, McGraw-Hill, 1968), pp. 266-267.

children accordingly. If grouping is to be effective, each child's profile and the manner of presentation which will work best for each youngster should be considered. Using this combination approach in grouping will realistically individualize instruction on those dimensions most crucial for effecting efficient learning. Instructional groups in classes for the retarded should not exceed two or three in a teaching-learning group to insure effective instruction. Administrators and school personnel can improve instruction, for retarded children by grouping children with similar problems and characteristics, rather than depending solely on achievement or labels. Quay's* framework provided a basis for grouping children according to their special needs in terms of educationally relevant variables rather than according to characteristics related to hypothetical causes or according to variables of concern to fields other than that of education. Thus, children can be grouped according to various defects which might be ameliorated by a particular instructional approach. Many characterists and defects among retarded children are similar; using this as a basis for grouping, administrators can place these children in an educational setting designed to increase their learning potentials.

Recently much dissatisfaction has been voiced against labeling and categorizing practices in special education. The general consensus is that labels do not present guides to effective educational treatment. Lord† wrote that we have established a fairly rigid grouping of children and many of these labels are not very descriptive of the children in these groups as we find them today. He stated that because of certain agencies and state support of programs based upon placement of students in categories, teacher training programs are forced to maintain current practices of categorizing exceptional children for funding purposes. In

---

*Herbert C. Quay, "The Facets of Educational Exceptionality: A Conceptual Framework for Assessing, Grouping, and Instruction," *Exceptional Children, 35*(1), (Sept. 1968), pp. 25-32.
†Francis E. Lord, "Medical Classification of Disabilities for Educational Purposes − A Critique," (Fifth Annual Distinguished Lecture Series in Special Education, Los Angeles, School of Education, University of Southern California, 1967), pp. 48-53.

support of Lord, Quay* inferred that many current disabilities categories have little educational utility. Hurley† related that there are many issues in education today but the hottest by far is the issue of labeling children and its corollary, the elimination of traditional categories of special education. Gallagher** stated that placing any label on any human being does violence to that individual uniqueness which is the joy of humanity. Yet, the practice is commonly done because it is such a convenient communication shorthand.

Most authorities generally agree that labeling children has created a list of descriptive words, such as defective, retarded, impaired, and disabled. Many of these descriptive words have been extended to retarded children. Frequently, these words have resulted in the formation of negative attitudes both in the children and the community at large. Much of the research in the field indicates that labels and classifications have little value for the school. The variability of the individual and the nonentity character of presumed homogenous groups require that school personnel look at the individual not as a mentally retarded child but as a unique individual with special needs. It is within the scope of the public school to eliminate, as much as possible, the use of labels for education purposes, which in many instances have proven unproductive and undemocratic in our society.

PROGRAM ADAPTATIONS

Variability within a group of retarded children in respect to physical, mental, social, and emotional growth and development is similar to that found among other groups of children. This means that the retarded differ from others not in kind, but in degree. Individually or as a group, they are not equally retarded in all intellectual activities or without varying strengths and weakness in

*Herbert Quay, *op. cit.,* pp. 25-32.
†L. O. Hurley, "A Categorical/Non-Categorical Issue: Implication for Teacher Trainers," (Columbia, Special Education Department, University of Missouri, 1971), pp. 39-40.
**J. J. Gallagher, "The Future Special Educational System," (The Missouri Conference on the Categorical/Non-Categorical Issue in Special Education, Columbia, University of Missouri Press, 1971), pp. 1-13.

other areas of growth. Yet their fundamental handicap of low mental capacity, coupled in many instances with other constitutional and environmental disabilities, reduces their chances for living a happy, satisfying life unless special provisions and techniques are provided by the schools for all ages. Degree of variability among retarded children become greater as they become older. Thus, the school should provide formal educational experiences for retarded children at an early age and program their learning in sequential steps throughout their school experiences. One of the basic means of achieving this end is through developing a functional curriculum based upon achievable objectives. The instructional process should encompass all the planned experiences provided by the school to assist pupils in attaining designated learning outcomes to the best of their abilities. It bridges the past, the present, and indicates future changes and needs mandatory in preparing an adequate way of life for the retarded in our society. Programs should be designed to develop and promote the child's mental, emotional, social, physical, and occupational needs and adjustment for the present as well as for the future. The changes in social forces, appraisal of instruction, and contribution of research should be combined for relevancy in educating the retarded. Program modification includes the understanding of retarded children, as individuals, an understanding of his home and community, in order to sequence educational tasks toward objectives.

Curriculum planners for programs dealing with retarded children should anticipate the shifts and changes in society and make curriculum relevant to those changes. Instruction for retarded children should be based on the nature of the children and of the society in which they live. Many retarded do not have access to many learning experiences that are common for other children, consequently, more than ordinary care must be taken to see that their experiences are feasible and realistic. Experiences offered retarded children should meet his short as well as long range needs. Administrators should be aware of the limitations of many retarded children to profit sufficiently from some school experiences, hence, many of the goals and objectives for them should be strongly based on the possible roles that they will assume in society. Activities should be sequenced so that realist goals and objectives can be achieved. They should be feasible for these children and relate to the roles that they may play in society. Modifications should be made in the instructional program as new societal trends and information dictate. School personnel should not be restricted from experimenting with a variety of activities in search for a program adapted to the needs, interests, and ability of retarded children.

The attainment of goals for retarded children basically is not different from other children, as long as realistic behavioral objectives are developed, based upon needs, characteristics, interests and ability of the retarded child in question. Equally important will be the assessment of areas where the retarded child can achieve some level of success, and to methodically sequence his educational experiences towards stated objectives. Program content must be individualized and modified to meet the unique needs of each child. No one instructional procedure can serve the needs of any group of retarded children. Moreover, the type of curriculum or instructional procedure used will greatly depend upon the observation of each child.

During the course of a school year, school personnel may need to request the consultative services of specialists in various disciplines. The integrated approach to learning, which is so necessary for the mentally retarded, requires that the services of specialists be coordinated and integrated with the work of the school. Joint participation of school and allied disciplines enables research and current finding in the field of mental retardation to become a part of daily classroom teaching.

If the schools are going to be committed to providing universal education for retarded children, special services must be provided in order that they might have equal educational opportunities. Many retarded children deviate so greatly in physical, mental, emotional, and cultural needs until special services and modification in the instructional program must be made if they are to attend school or to profit from its instruction. The schools have not been very effective in serving many of the needs of retarded children. Ross* charged that the educational system has

---

*Sterling L. Ross, Henry G. DeYong, and Julius S. Cohen, "Confrontation: Special Education Placement and the Law," *Exceptional Children, 38*(1), (September), p. 5.

consistently ignored pleas for change to make school experience more relevant to children who may be neither highly motivated nor achievement oriented or who come from culturally different backgrounds. Goldberg* reflected that the schools can more effectively serve the retarded child if a thorough assessment of his abilities and disabilities is made and that the retarded has the right to be placed in a learning environment opportunity with his educational diagnoses. Providing special services to the retarded should not be misconstrued by the schools as a social service, but as fulfilling the educational rights of retarded children as mandated under our constitution.

FINANCIAL PROVISIONS

The cost of an adequate educational program for the mentally retarded requires special allocations to be made in the school budget.

An adequately enriched program for the mentally retarded necessitates a financial outlay that is proportionately greater than that for normal children. The materials and equipment needed for the practical experiences of these children are expensive when provided in sufficient quantity and variety. Proper education for the retarded require higher per capita expenditure than for the nonhandicapped. Federal, state and local governments should provide financial support to improve the educational opportunities of retarded children. Otherwise, schools are in danger of being inadequately and poorly staffed. Moreover, the total program is likely to suffer. Only by making special allocations in the school budget for retarded children is there assurance that needed funds will not be diverted to other purposes.

It is doubtful that local school systems can design comprehensive programs for the retarded without the aid of external financial support. Through federal and state support and grants, school districts will be motivated to improve and develop new programs for serving retarded children. The high cost of educating the mentally retarded can be justified when the consequences to the community are not providing a suitable education for them are

*I. Ignacy Goldberg, "Human Rights for the Mentally Retarded in the School System," *Mental Retardation,* 9(6), (December, 1971), p. 6.

considered. A community that neglects the mentally retarded is likely to pay a higher price later for crime, unemployment, welfare relief, and delinquency that stem largely from a lack of proper education. In the long run, a good school program for retarded children, whatever its cost, is cheaper than the price of neglect.

The school should be cognizant of other provisions that require financial support, over and beyond that required for normal children, such as transportation, physical plant, supplies and equipment, individualized instructional programs, and supportive services and personnel. If the democratic principles of education are to be realized for these children, it is incumbent that financial consideration be given to the above without additional financial burden to parents or guardians of retarded children. School districts should not have to be petitioned to provide quality educational opportunities for retarded children which are already guaranteed under their democratic rights.

One of the most expensive outlays in providing quality education for retarded children is that of securing teaching and supportive personnel. The success of any administrative organization will depend greatly upon the abilities of personnel on all levels. Many of the personnel serving retarded children must have specialized training. This trend will accentuate the cost of educating retarded children beyond that required for normal children. Administrators should work for facilities and trained personnel adequate for diagnosing and for teaching the mentally retarded. Retarded children must be educated at the levels of their abilities and by methods and techniques fitted to their needs. Future usefulness and need should be the basis for instruction, regardless of the price tag.

Without skilled administrators it is not likely that retarded children will benefit significantly from their school experiences. In a 1970 survey by Bullock* it was revealed that none of the 50 states, the District of Columbia, or Puerto Rico required a single course in special education within the certification requirements for school principals. Other findings were that of 92 elementary principals, 65 percent, had elected no course work in special

---

*L. Bullock, "An Inquiry into the Special Education Training of Elementary School Administrators," *Exceptional Children, 36,* (Summer, 1970), pp. 770-1.

education, 33 percent had one course in special education, 50 percent had taken two or more courses in the field. The gravity of the situation is that the principal is the key person in providing quality education for retarded children. It becomes crucial when educational leadership is not conducted by qualified and competent personnel. Without academic training principals can not possibly understand the needs and attitudes of retarded children. The school is derelict in its duty when it does not insist upon adequately trained personnel to serve the many needs of retarded children.

In summary, the functions and responsibilities of the school in providing services to the retarded are complex. The school must be willing to adapt to the realities of the time and to cooperate with other agencies in the community in order to affect present as well as future changes brought about as a result of our complex society, innovation in the field, and improved technology. Quality education for retarded children mandates that the school work cooperatively with other agencies for better ways and methods of identifying retarded children at an early age, to assess their needs, and from the assessed needs develop relevant instructional procedures. Equally important will be the utilization of proper resources and facilities, coordinating activities in the community, and evaluating success of the program based upon realistic objectives. In a democratic society, the schools should assume the responsibility for educating retarded as well as all other children. Unless special provisions are made for retarded children it is not likely that they will profit sufficiently from instruction. It should be the responsibility of the school to guarantee that the human rights of the retarded will not be abridged by failing to offer services and provisions commensurate with their abilities.

CHAPTER 4

IS SEGREGATION VS. INTEGRATION THE ISSUE?

SOME authorities support the notion that integration provides the best approach for educating educable retarded children, others maintain that children can obtain their optimum growth in a special class, and still others advocate that the issue is not integration versus segregation, but whether appropriate goals, instructional procedures, and supportive services exist for these children.

At this point, it might be appropriate to review some of the factors involved in the creation of special education programs for retarded children. Special education programs were not initiated in response to the needs of exceptional children, but rather as an expedient measure to resist a perceived threat to existing goals for "normal" children. Parent movements pressured public schools to accept their children who had been excluded from schools for various reasons* and hence forced the schools to initiate special education programs so as to avoid disturbing the establishment. Consequently, special education programs were initiated. A stated or unstated purpose of such classes was to develop within the pupil basic attitudes, habits, and skills which would enable him to adjust to and live in our increasingly complex society. Basic to the achievement of this goal was the ability of the pupils to use these attitudes, habits, and skills in securing and holding a job.†

Special educators in general took great pride and satisfaction in the rapid expansion of special education programs. The most commonly stated goal of special education programs is to meet the needs of exceptional children whose needs are not being

---

*M. C. Reynolds, "The Surge in Special Education," *National Education Association,* 56, (Nov., 1967), pp. 46-48.

†Dorothy D. Dawes, *et. al., Occupational Education,* (Philadelphia, Philadelphia Public School Printing Office, 1963).

adequately met in regular programs (Baker, 1959). Much of the controversy exists because many specialists now generally agree that the special class model or goals, which have been in existence well over thirty years, have not provided mentally retarded children with a viable education. Thus, criticisms begin to emerge from several sources, questioning the justification of special education programs with a plea that special educators stop being pressured to continue and expand a special education program that is known to be undesirable for many of the children we are dedicated to serve.* It was further voiced that throughout the number of years special education programs have been in operation, research findings have consistently indicated no differences in performance between those placed in regular classes opposed to those placed in special classes.

Proponents for special classes replied that there has been no reliable evidence produced to indicate that either social or academic benefits accrue to children as a result of being placed in a regular class. Thus, the issue "integration versus segregation" was launched. In order to review the research in an objective manner, it might be profitable to separate the research into two areas, "integration versus segregation."

THE INTEGRATED APPROACH

Those in favor of integrated classes agreed that (1) they conformed more closely to democratic values and principles; (2) the mentally retarded child would profit both academically and socially from opportunities for frequent association with normal children; (3) the normal child would acquire a better understanding of and a greater respect for individual differences; (4) parents tend to devalue their children to a greater degree in special classes when compared to regular classes; (5) labeling not only influences the retarded child's perception of his own abilities, but also affects his actual abilities; and (6) once segregation becomes institutionalized it is most difficult to eliminate.

The academic consequences of special class placement on

*Lloyd Dunn, "Special Education for the Mildly Retarded — Is Much of It Justifiable?," *Exceptional Children, 35,* (Sept., 1968), p. 5.

educable retarded children have not proven significant.* At times a slight advantage from regular class placement for academic skills and a slight advantage from special class placement for social emotional adjustment has been found. In both settings educable retardates were not achieving at their optimum levels. In support of this premise, a survey conducted by the U.S. Office of Education† found no clear support for either regular or special placement in terms of academic achievement; the only exceptions were found when personality variables such as achievement motivation or anxiety factors were considered. The afore-mentioned research can be summarized by stating that educable retardates appear to function academically at a higher level in regular classes.

The possibility of attitudinal effects on parents whose children have been given special class placement should not be minimized.** Research findings revealed that parents of EMR children in special classes generally showed greater awareness of their child's retardation but tended to devalue their child to a greater degree than did parents of EMR children in regular classes. It was concluded that special classes may lead, in the long run to maladaptive behavior.

Considering the overall picture of research evidence supporting integration, the following guidelines might be useful in planning for educable retarded chidren. First, it should be recognized that the adjustment of the retarded child to the normal world is unlikely to occur unless he has frequent and familiar interaction with it. The risk that such interaction may contribute to a greater maladjustment of the retarded is undeniable, yet adequate adjustment is dependent on taking such risks. The importance of contact with a broad spectrum of students will enable the retarded child to function in a world beyond the school, a world without the segregated protection of the school. Segregated special classes

---

*W. Baldwin, "The Social Position of the Educable Retarded Child in the Regular Grades in the Public School," *Exceptional Children, 25,* (Nov., 1958), pp. 106-12.
†June Franseth and Rose Koury, *"Survey of Research on Grouping as Related to Pupil Learning,"* (Washington, D. C., U.S. Printing Office, 1966).
**J. H. Meyerowitz, "Parental Awareness of Retardation," *American Journal of Mental Deficiency, 71* (Jan., 1967), pp. 637-43.

reduce the contact of regular students with handicapped students, and this impedes the development of positive attitudes on the part of regular students, and thus special education may be creating new problems in trying to solve old ones.

Secondly, another significant point used against special classes as outlined by proponents of integration is that of "labeling." The following point is advanced, when students are grouped and labeled according to some characteristic believed to relate to their ability to profit from education, that label becomes an explanation for their behavior. Such easy access to explanations for failure can serve to reduce efforts for improved educational practices. There is some evidence that such grouping and labeling not only influences the student perception of his own abilities, but it also affects his actual abilities.*

Thirdly, once segregation becomes institutionalized, it is most difficult to eliminate. Any initial steps toward educational segregation should therefore be cautious, and adequately supported by research before wide implementation is initiated. The difficulty is magnified if current special education programs are administratively well-entrenched and continue to multiply, giving rise to the real danger that the primary goal of special education may become self-perpetuation. The above pointers are but a few of the justifications that supporters of integration have advanced.

THE SEGREGATION APPROACH

Proponents of segregated education for the mentally retarded maintained that, (1) administratively and pedagogically the special school could provide more efficient and higher quality services; (2) the application of auxiliary services such as psychology, guidance, and speech would be facilitated; (3) the absence of an "unhealthy" competitive environment would be both academically and emotionally beneficial to children poorly equipped to compete; (4) the fact that an educable retarded child is in a special class is to a large extent dependent upon previous

*R. Rosenthal and L. Jacobson, "Teachers Expectancies: Determiners of Pupils' Gains," *Psychological Report, 19,* (August, 1966), pp. 115-118.

teacher rejection; (5) the harmful effects of special class placement have not been scientifically demonstrated; (6) if there is no segregation of deviant individuals — all deviant individuals being assigned to regular classes, we are setting the goal of teaching to the mean; and (7) special class placement is sought only for those who need management beyond that possible in the regular classroom. *

Advocates of special classes maintain that special class placement may save some youngsters from psychological damage. Without the special class possibility, rejected retarded children might have no place to escape.

Supporters of special classes state that the values and attitudes of teachers and their effects on pupils self-perception and performances are the key questions. Segregation without a program is just as destructive as integration without understanding. Returning to an education system which ignores the promise and possibility of the special class would disregard the imperatives of educational history, which have mandated an alternative to wide range heterogeneity.

Concerning the question of research findings, proponents of special classes agree that findings appear to indicate that grouping handicapped children together has no beneficial effect upon them. This is used as an argument for abolishing special classes for all kinds of children. Yet, the harmful effects of special classes have not been demonstrated. It is commonly agreed that present methods of measurement are not sensitive enough to register changes in placement, therefore the results supporting regular classes are inconclusive and not based or conducted on scientific principles.

The segregationists state if there is no segregation of deviant individuals — all deviant individuals being assigned to regular classes, we are setting the goal of teaching to the mean. Using this

*I. Goldberg and L. Blackman, "The Special Class: Parastic, Edophytic, Symbiotic Cell in Body Pedagogic," *Mental Retardation*, 3(1), (April, 1965), pp. 30-31.

Peter Valletutti, *op. cit.,* pp. 405-408.

Mary Engel, "The Tin Drum Revisited," *The Journal of Special Education*, 3(4), (Winter, 1969), p. 385.

format, the educable retarded would do poorly, the slow learner would benefit to some degree, the average child would do fairly well, and the gifted would learn that it was not productive or popular to do too much or even too well. This rationale supports special classes because it indicates that the exceptional child is one who needs special management. Proponents state that they are seeking special class placement only for those who need management beyond that possible in the regular classroom. The common consensus, according to people who advocate special classes is that critics often ignore the fact that special class placement is often very beneficial to the educable mentally retarded, and other handicapped children.

ADMINISTRATIVE CONCERNS

Administrators should weigh the placement factors with as much objectivity as possible before accepting any plan for placing retarded children. Programming for retarded children can be facilitated, regardless of the plan selected, if the following are adhered: (1) clearly defined goals and objectives, (2) sequenced instructional tasks, (3) well-trained personnel, (4) supportive services, and (5) community and parental support.

CLEARLY DEFINED GOALS AND OBJECTIVES

When there is no consensus on goals and/or objectives there is no logical means for choosing one approach over another, one kind of staff over another, one program component over another. It would not make sense to initiate an experimental effort unless goals or objectives were made explicit and a set of priorities chosen.* Clearly stated educational goals for retarded children should do much to minimize the conflict in the field. An avoidance of clearly stated goals allows educators to verbally support appropriate programs. If clearly beneficial objectives, unique for a particular exceptionality, cannot be identified, then

---

*Lam Empey, "Alternative to Incarceration," (Washington, D. C., H.E.W., Office of Juvenile Delinquency and Youth Development, 1967).

the exceptional group in question should not be segregated from normal society or regular classes. It is true that while behavioral objectives of classroom instruction have been fairly well defined in most areas of exceptionality, for the retarded child they are often vaguely stated. Clearly defined objectives will emphasize accepted behaviors of children as well as skills and activities needed to reach the objectives.

To achieve these goals for retardates, administrators should have specific objectives in mind as well as some plan for sequencing steps or tasks that will lead to desired behaviors. There are several steps that administrators may take to assure that objectives and goals are met:

1. Understanding and categorizing the objectives of the school's curriculum.

2. Defining the objectives or goals in terms of expected behavior, based upon observable and measurable data.

3. Developing instruments, materials and activities to assess or determine if desired behaviors have been met.

4. Instituting changes at any point in the instructional process if it appears that objectives are not being met.

5. Sequencing tasks where retarded children can experience success, this will involve moving from known experiences to unknown, and concrete experiences to levels of abstraction.

Application of these steps will allow administrators to achieve one of the chief objectives of the school, the promotion of learning. It is almost impossible to gauge how successful an instructional program has been unless objectives are first clearly and concisely stated.

SEQUENCED INSTRUCTIONAL TASKS

Another crucial problem that administrators face before they elect to choose a plan for their retarded children is that of sequencing instructional tasks. Ingram* pointed out that special education must consider the value for out-of-school life adjustment of what they are teaching. In essence what will the

*T. T. S. Ingram, "Education — For What Purpose?," In J. Loring, Ed., *Teaching the Cerebral Palsied,* (Lavenham, Suffolk, England, Lavenham Press, Ltd., 1965), pp. 1-3.

final product be? Before a plan is adopted those behaviors which he must master for successful living must be identified and programmed in sequencial steps for the goals and instruction to be useful. These procedural changes should take priority over segregation versus integration.

Not many of new curricula have been developed for retarded children. More effective tools to measure the characteristics of retarded pupils must be developed, and the development of curricula in line with these unique patterns. The emphasis will be placed on needs and characteristics, rather than placement. The curriculum for the mentally retarded would be based upon realistic goals and approaches. These approaches in turn should be formulated on the basis of needs, capacities and interests.

Individual differences and program scope must be recognized when planning an instructional program for retarded children. Program scope includes the totality of experiences and activities to which an individual is exposed during a specified period of time. Therefore, teachers must be skilled in informal assessment procedures so that both the general and specific characteristics of the children can be described and reacted to in the instructional program.

The evaluation of an instructional program should include evidence that the program has or has not reached its objectives and should also provide the basis for conclusions and recommendations for improving the program. All relevant data should be matched or developed to meet the program's objectives; data and information not germane to the objectives should not be included in the instructional process.

Recognition by the school of the mentally retarded child as a whole, from the time of his identification to the time of his discharge, would seem to warrant methods of instruction that take into account all of his general and specific behaviors. These behaviors would include the development of desirable general personality characteristics and the acquisition of specific knowledge and skills that should emulate from the instructional program. In essence the instructional program should be directly associated with the goals and objectives as set forth.

By developing goals on a continuum of levels of difficulty, a two-fold purpose is accomplished. First, the teacher is assisted in establishing objectives for each class in such a way that they are sequential in an ascending order of difficulty and are also achievable in a forseeable future. Second, because individual capabilities and competencies vary among children with comparable measurable abilities, such a sequence permits some to move further and faster than others in a single class.

Since most goals for the retarded children are essentially short range in contrast with the traditional concept of short- and long-range plans for those with more normal, intellectual ability, it becomes increasingly important for the stated objectives to be precise and clear cut. In addition, there needs to be frequent evaluation of progress made, together with a review of the estimate of the child's potential in relation to his attainment. Finally, it is important that the limited capacity for growth and learning of mentally retarded children not be dissipated in meaningless or unproductive activity.

TRAINED PERSONNEL

Professional preparation of school personnel is desperately needed. High standards are needed for the selection of directors, supervisors, and teachers of educable retarded children to achieve stated goals. Ideally, before placing a special child in any class, the training, attitudes, and values of the teacher should be carefully and precisely delineated. Discovering the pupil's characteristics which a given teacher will accept or reject becomes a critical administrative question. The nature of the teacher's response to expressed hostility, physical attributes, and academic skill should be included in the placement decision. Questions of this nature are critical and have more relevancy than integration versus segregation. Solutions are not easy, but revisions in teacher training programs are clearly a priority. All teachers must be trained to seek, identify and demand the assistance needed to educate the retarded.

One assumption underlying the preparation of teachers of the retarded is that these teachers should stress somewhat different goals than those designed for the child in a regular classroom.* Robinson and Robinson† stated that such an approach is necessary since stressing academic accomplishments would be inappropriate to most of these children. They expressed that the special classes have primarily been designed to enhance the development of the retarded child's social competencies, personal adequacy, and occupational skills. Research tends to support the notion that special class teachers place greater emphasis upon personal and social adjustment than did regular class teachers and also appeared to demand less in the way of achievement from the low ability child.** In support of this premise Schmidt and Nelson†† conducted a study concerned with the cognitive/affective dimensions considered basic to the effectiveness of a special class teacher working with educable retarded pupils. They concluded that special class teachers consider personal and social adjustment of major importance when compared to subject matter acquisition.

Johnson¶ identified teachers' low expectations of retarded children as a prime factor in the present controversy. The preceding statement perhaps can be attributed to the lack of teacher preparation in educating retarded individuals. Universities and colleges must share some of the blame for teachers who are not adequately prepared to teach retardates. Radical models in teacher education must be developed to off-set this trend. Sellin§

---

*L. F. Cain, "The Teacher and the Handicapped Child," *Education*, 1949, 69, pp. 275-279.

M. L. Hutt and R. G. Gibby, *The Mentally Retarded Child: Development, Education and Treatment,* 2nd Ed., (Boston: Allyn & Bacon, 1965).

†H. B. Robinson and N. M. Robinson, *The Mentally Retarded Child: A Psychological Approach,* (New York: McGraw-Hill, 1965).

**M. J. Fine, "Attitudes of Regular and Special Class Teachers Towards the Educable Mentally Retarded Child," *Exceptional Children, 33*(6), (Feb., 1967), pp. 429-30.

C. C. Nelson, "Affective and Cognitive Attitudes of Junior High School Teachers and Pupils," *The Journal of Educational Research,* (58), (Oct., 1967), pp. 81-83.

††Leo J. Schmidt and Calvin C. Nelson, "The Affective/Cognitive Attitude Dimension of Teachers of Educable Mentally Retarded Minors," *Exceptional Children, 35*(9), (May, 1969), pp. 695-701.

¶ G. O. Johnson, "Special Education for the Mentally Handicapped – A Paradox," *Exceptional Children, 29,* (Oct., 1962), pp. 62-9.

§ Donald F. Sellin, "Mental Retardation 1984: Will the Paradox End?," *Mental Retardation, 9*(4), (August, 1971), pp. 34-35.

proposed that a lack of a definition of professionalism is the issue in teacher preparation. He stated that a commitment to a definition of professionalism would rally points for united efforts among professors, administrators, practitioners, and concerned citizens.

Preparation for administrators of special education programs for retardates should include; (a) a minimum of five years of satisfactory teaching experience in a class for mentally retarded children; (b) a baccalaureate degree with at least 30 graduate course credits in education, supervision, problems of the retarded, psychology and sociology; (c) to manifest competence an administrator should be able to meet approved standards in written tests, and demonstrations; and (d) a physical test should be passed and the administrator's records and experiences evaluated.* Since the problems of retarded children are so extensive and intricate, it is recommended that administrators be trained on an interdisciplinary basis. Institutions of higher learning must develop models whereas training will cut across all disciplines. Training based solely on an educational model is too narrow to produce effective administrators. Models should be developed in line with community services. Through a coordination of efforts, institutions can effect training programs that are relevant and field based, where students must demonstrate their skills in a variety of community agencies concerned with serving the retarded. In-service programs should be designed to upgrade the skills of all school personnel working with the retarded.

SUPPORTIVE SERVICES

If proper supportive services are not provided for retarded children no degree of placement will be effective. Special helping teachers, itinerant, or school-based, resource rooms, and other well-known educational manipulations are needed if any plan is to be successful. Retarded children generally have many handicaps that a teacher can not manage alone, such as speech disorders, defective hearing, poor reading ability, weak vision, and behavioral

---

*Harold Fields, "Selecting Supervisors for the Mentally Retarded," *Journal of Exceptional Children, 22,* (March, 1956), p. 224.

maladjustments are a few of the existing difficulties. Conversely, the services of many specialists will be needed to promote better pupil growth and adjustment.

COMMUNITY AND PARENTAL SUPPORT

It would be neglectful not to explore the role and dimensions of the community and parental support. A desirable relationship between school and community is one that is marked by a strong bond of understanding and cooperation between parents and school personnel. Parents should have a direct share in deciding what plan of placement appears to service their children best. Parents should be welcome to make suggestions for the guidance of their children. Through various channels the school can interpret its program for retarded children and enlist the cooperation of parents and the community.

The issue at hand should not be integration versus segregation, but whether there are appropriate goals, curricula, personnel, supportive services, and mutual support and acceptance of the plan advanced.

CHAPTER 5

CAN WE INSURE CONTINUOUS PROGRESS FOR RETARDED CHILDREN?

 T HE growth and development of the mentally retarded should be supported by a school policy of continuous pupil progress involving supportive services and community support. A flexibility of organization and a spirit of teamwork characterize a school that permits readjustment of mentally retarded children whenever necessary. Generally, the schools have tended to neglect retarded children by not tailoring instruction to their unique needs. These children need specialized help if they are going to be contributing members of our society. The key is early identification, a programmed sequence geared towards their needs, and support from community and parents.

ASSESSING NEEDS

Stafford* outlined that the diagnostic process should involve more than intellectual assessment; it should cover the total needs of the child, encompassing many of the behavioral areas, depending upon the child's disabilities. Information gained from the diagnostic evaluation should be consolidated to form a profile of the child, depicting his liabilities as well as strengths. Specialists should be available to interpret the diagnostic data to school personnel, because of the lack of interpretation. Concerns about the evaluation of handicapped children have perplexed school personnel and other related professional workers for some time. Often psychometric data have not been translated into applicable educational terms, thus many professionals have rejected outright

---

*Richard L. Stafford and Roger J. Meyer, "Diagnosis and Counseling for the Mentally Retarded: Implications for School Health," *The Journal of School Health, 38*(3), (March, 1968), pp. 151-155.

the whole idea of testing; their common consensus being that much of the psychometric data have been used only to label children. Weiner's* solution is that more thought be given to systematic observation procedures applied in the classroom or other life situations. Similarly, Schwartz† enumerated that clinical type education capable of providing diagnosis and remediation programs to meet the needs of exceptional children is expanding rapidly. It was proposed that curricula approaches be changed to assist teachers in becoming skilled diagnosticians. Any information gathered or received by the teacher concerning retarded children, if properly used can facilitate the instructional process.

There are many devices that administrators can suggest that teachers employ to supplement diagnostic evaluation, and to assist in evaluating the effectiveness of their educational programs. First, audio-visual aids, including films, slides, video tapes, pictures, and television have been used to assess progress of children. If the diagnostic evaluation indicates poor motor control, children's initial respond to a planned remedial program which might be taped and compared with later tapes to denote progress. Second, rating scales have been successfully used by teachers to measure student's behavior in various areas. Observation from rating scales will yield valuable information about the child's abilities and disabilities which can be programmed into the instructional program. Rating scales and/or checklists constructed and administered by teachers can assist in determining to what extent the goals of the program have been fulfilled. Third, developmental scales are useful devices that teachers can be trained to use to determine individual progress, growth, and development.

There is a pressing need to include demonstrations of various diagnostic devices and the procedures to construct and/or administer them by teachers of retardates. Workshops, seminars, institutes, professional meetings, and college level courses stressing the use of diagnostic devices will facilitate the teacher's

---

*Bluma B. Weiner, "Assessment: Beyond Psychometry," *Exceptional Children, 33*(6) (February, 1967), pp. 367-370.

†Louis Schwartz, "An Integrated Teacher Education Program for Special Education – A New Approach," *Exceptional Children, 33*(6), (February, 1967), pp. 411-16.

understanding of diagnostic evaluation, as well as provide him with useful information that can be programmed into the instructional program. Diagnosis of the needs of the retarded, to a large extent, must depend upon the perceptive teacher employing his own observational skills.

CONTINUOUS ASSESSMENT AND PROGRAM DEVELOPMENT

Programming should begin the day the child is considered for special education and continue step by step in terms of the behavioral clues observed in the child. The administrator and his faculty promote better human relationships by assisting the mentally retarded in learning to get along with others, practicing good work habits, and developing adequate health habits. Through carefully planned routines each child learns, to the extent of his ability, to form acceptable concepts for living. The emerging program is modified and constantly evaluated in terms of the personality of each child in relation to his parents, to school personnel, and to other people with whom he comes in contact.*

Retarded children should not be expected to achieve the usual grade standards as their peers. Their curriculum is based upon their individual needs and revolves around meaningful, practical problems of living. They can advance from one group to the next on the basis of social maturity and chronological age rather than academic achievement. School organization should not hinder the promotion or transfer of mentally retarded children from one group to another. These children should be moved naturally, without failure and anxiety, within the school organization. Thus they will always be members of a compatible group that promotes their best growth and development. Ease of transfer, promotion, and even exclusion when necessary, require the full cooperation and understanding of teachers, parents, principals, and supervisors. Each educator considers the good of

*Bernice Baumgartner, *Guiding the Retarded Child*, (New York: The John Day Company, 1956), pp. 16-17.

the child as the major criterion when decisions concerning progress have to be made. The school policy should permit whatever is best for the mentally retarded to be done without hindrance. Continuous pupil progress is increased by cooperation within and between various administrative and teaching units.

IMPROVING EDUCATIONAL PROVISIONS
FOR THE RETARDED

Special education should function within and as a part of the regular public school framework. Within this framework, the function of special education should be to participate in the creation and maintenance of a total educational environment, suitable for all children. From their base in the regular school system special educators can foster the development of specialized resources by coordinating their specialized contributions with the contributions of the regular school system. One of the primary goals of special educators should be the enhancement of regular class programs as a resource for all children.*

Continuous assessment and programming require trained personnel to conduct a quality program for retarded children. Olson and Hahn† analyzed and described a special approach to preparing teachers of the mentally retarded. They recommended that undergraduate teacher candidates need the following experiences: (a) a sound general education with emphasis in the behavioral sciences, (b) early exposure to the field of special education, (c) instruction in curriculum and teaching methodology, and (d) the opportunity to observe excellence in teaching. They would assign particular emphasis to observation and practice teaching experience. Direct observations should be carefully arranged to include observation of excellent teachers in action followed by a seminar in which the professor and university student can jointly evaluate what was observed. These demonstrations might take place in public school classrooms, in university demonstration classes, and, under certain conditions, in

*Policy Statements: *Exceptional Children,* 1971, *op. cit.,* pp. 183-184.
†James L. Olson and Hans R. Hahn, "One Approach to Preparing Teachers of the Mentally Retarded," *High School Journal, 48,* (Dec., 1964), pp. 191-7.

university classrooms where the curriculum methods course is taught. During the last phase of teacher preparation, students would be assigned to full-time student teaching with provision for weekly seminars concentrating on problems encountered during the teaching day.

Wolinsky* analyzed aspects of a teacher education program for teachers preparing to work with trainable children. She recommended three areas that should be incorporated in such a program: (1) adequate foundation in developmental psychology, including emphasis on laboratory experiences, and the case-study approach; (2) acquaintance with basic skills, and insights of other disciplines involved with exceptional children; and (3) awareness of basic principles of counseling and interviewing.

The education of the mentally retarded is so important to the welfare of society that the very best teachers are needed. Wholesome personality traits are desirable, such as patience, a sense of humor, emotional stability, much energy, friendliness, adaptability, and a sincere but no sentimental interest in the mentally retarded are but a few factors to be considered in selecting teachers. Whatever the procedure for selection, teachers who are appointed should be those able to give mentally retarded children the best educational opportunities possible for happy, successful living.

In most school systems the administrators are in a key position to facilitate or retard changes and innovations. Whereas a principal alone once held the responsibility for the education of the mentally retarded, he now coordinates his efforts with those of one or more supervisors in order to facilitate programming for the retarded. Administrators should have teaching experiences with retarded children as well as graduate training which should include courses from several disciplines. Training for administrators should not be terminal; they should attend workshops, seminars, symposiums, and take in-service courses to keep abreast with the many changes in the field. High standards are needed for the selection of directors, principals, and supervisors of special

---

*Gloria F. Wolinsky, "Theoretical and Practical Aspects of a Teacher Education Program for Teachers of the Trainable Child," *American Journal of Mental Deficiency, 63,* (May, 1959), pp. 948-53.

education programs for the mentally retarded. With the selection of the most capable administrators possible, teachers of retardates can be given maximum help in achieving the goals of education for these children.

Educational administration should provide the means for enhancing the teacher-learning process. A climate conducive to professional growth should be provided whereby the teaching personnel feel they are productive members in the improvement of instruction and the development of programs for retarded children. No administrator can effectively plan an instructional program for retarded children without the aid and support of the teaching staff; therefore, it is of prime importance that there be total involvement and participation of all concerned with the education of the retarded. Total involvement and participation does not negate complete accord between the administration and teaching staff concerning philosophies and educational practices, or how an instructional program will operate. Administrators should recognize individual beliefs and work to reduce discrepancies in their units, in order that the goals and objectives of the program can be met.

It is important that teachers of children with a mental handicap have the support and guidance of administrators who are well informed concerning the needs, interests, and abilities of the mentally retarded. A modern program of supervision based on sound educational principles enables these teachers to gain deeper understanding of the factors and principles underlying and influencing their practices. They are helped to examine their professional actions critically to see if the purposes of education for the mentally retarded are being met effectively. The effect of supervision by competent, adequately prepared administrators and supervisors will be improvement of the total teaching-learning situations for the mentally retarded.

IMPROVED SERVICES

In this present century, services to retarded children have increased considerably. This increase can perhaps be attributed to many factors such as: demands from local and national groups, increases in funds from the state and local levels, the federal government, private interests in research, and improved inter-disciplinary communications. These trends have highlighted the need for additional services to meet the needs of retarded children in many ways such as, improved relations between community agencies and the schools, transportation facilities, specialized equipment, improved teaching techniques, and adding supportive personnel to the school staff. Administrators responsible for programming for retarded children should make full use of existing facilities in the community, seek additional funds to hire supportive personnel, or ask for volunteers from various agencies to support the school programs, and investigate the plausibility of incorporating new teaching devices such as programmed instruction in their program. It should be generally recognized that providing special services to retarded children is expensive and complex, and therefore, will require the combined efforts of many agencies and groups.

It has been commonly stated that no effective program can operate successfully for retarded children unless there is common understanding between various segments of the community and parents. All necessary information concerning the education of the child should be made available to the parent. Parents and the community should have direct input into the development of a special education program. For administrators and related school personnel, programming should involve the utilization of information from parents and community.

The involvement of community agencies is needed to improve guidance, rehabilitation, and the general educational opportunities of retarded children. The principal becomes the key person by coordinating activities between the school and community. There are many local, state, and federal agencies that can provide needed services for the retarded. Locally, the Division of Vocational Rehabilitation might provide testing and evaluation of potential employees. Goodwill Industries and other community based programs might provide sheltered employment. State employment agencies frequently work with the schools to improve job opportunities for retarded children and youth. The federal government through its Division of Vocational Rehabilitation and the Economic Opportunity Act, provides funds to employees to pay retardates on a part-time basis, until proper skills are learned for the job. Due to various community health projects financed by the federal government, there are a number of agencies that are providing special clinical services to help the retarded. The cooperation between the schools and community will enable administrators to plan systematically for each retarded child's growth from grade school through post-school living.

FLEXIBILITY IN PLACEMENT

The mentally retarded should be assigned to classes that are organized to foster maximum pupil growth and development.

When identification has been made by careful diagnostic procedures, mentally retarded children should be placed as soon as possible in a class that is likely to meet their unique needs. The common consensus is that children with special educational needs be educated in regular classrooms if their needs can adequately be met, or to provide supplementary services for those children who cannot benefit from the regular school program. Based on the needs of the individual child, it might be necessary to remove retarded children from certain types of educational settings within the public schools, and place them in residential schools, hospitals, or various training programs in the community.

Historically, administrators in the area of special education have assumed that a child who was mentally retarded should be placed in a segregated setting where he would have a chance for success with intellectually comparable peers. Advocates of special classes for educable children have contended that among other advantages, these classes promote in the children the acquisition of a more realistic and healthy self-concept. Conversely, some studies have shown no improvement in academic progress of retarded children in special classes when compared with retarded children in regular classes. Other studies comparing class placement of educable mentally retardates have produced conflicting results as to which placement contributes to greater academic achievement and a better self-concept.* These studies compounded with recent research have created a controversy in the field of special education concerning placement.† (Chapter 4 covers the controversy of placement in detail).

A TOTAL APPROACH

Administrative personnel can insure continuous progress for retardates by providing a systematic program with assessment and re-assessment of each child's abilities for his total school experiences. The schools are not equipped to provide this service alone, but will need the combined support of many agencies and disciplines. Realistic goals and objectives must be stated in concise terms. Educational tasks must be sequenced to permit the child to receive some measure of success in his academic pursuits. Tasks should be sequenced to serve the child's immediate as well as his long-range needs. To achieve this end, administrators should incorporate the educational program with comprehensive community services and related agencies dealing with training and certification of administrators and teaching personnel.

Institutions responsible for the preparation of teaching personnel, college professors, state departments of education, the public schools, and other groups are too fragmented and appear to be working in opposite directions. In order to insure continuous progress for the retarded, acceptable standards of competencies are needed for all teaching personnel, combined with professional education legislated at the state level addressed to such standards. These standards should be administered by educators representing all personnel concerned with educating retarded children.

---

*Anne W. Carrol, "The Effects of Segregated and Partially Integrated School Programs on Self-Concept and Academic Achievement of EMR," *Exceptional Children, 34*, (Oct., 1967), pp. 93-99.

S. H. Ainsworth, *"An Exploratory Study of Educational, Social, and Emotional Factors on the Education of Mentally Retarded Children in Georgia Public Schools,"* (Cooperative Research Project Report, N. 171 (6470) Washington, D.C., USOE, 1959).

B. Blatt, "The Physical, Personality, and Academic Status of Children Who are Mentally Retarded Attending Regular Classes," *American Journal of Mental Deficiency, 62*, (March, 1958), pp. 810-18.

†I. Goldberg and L. Blackman, *op. cit.*, pp. 30-31.

A major function of the school is to recognize each pupil as a unique individual and to help each one develop his abilities to the fullest. The educational program must, therefore, take carefully into account the individual differences among pupils. Administrators and school personnel, adequately trained, can assist the school in reaching this basic goal. Programming for retarded children involves the commitment of the total school and community, as well as supportive service and programs to meet their many needs.*

---

*George R. Taylor, "Programming for EMR Children," *Training School Bulletin, 67*(3), (November, 1970), pp. 183-188.

CHAPTER 6

HOW SHOULD SCHOOL ACHIEVEMENT BE EVALUATED?

THE progress of mentally retarded children should be carefully and regularly evaluated and reported. The continuous appraisal of their progress toward the goals and objectives discloses strengths and weaknesses of behavior and achievement and indicates what guidance and experiences need to be given. Evaluation gives opportunities for reassuring the mentally retarded of their progress, bolstering their confidence in themselves and providing needed satisfaction.

Effective evaluation includes identifying, observing, measuring, and analyzing various aspects of the retardate's performance in light of established goals. The establishment of well-defined goals must include the expected behavior that students will display as a result of the instructional program. If students do not meet expected goals or objectives, teachers and administrators should examine the instructional program; the interests, needs, and abilities of the students; and the adequacy of the goals themselves. The next step would be to rewrite goals and objectives in light of the needs, interests, and abilities of the group.

OBSERVING AND RECORDING

Evidence in evaluating the progress of pupils can be collected from many sources and situations, both individual and group, in which the members of the class function. All the improvisions made by the children as they communicate or express themselves through sound, writing, or the arts are utilized. Anecdotal records which give descriptions of child behavior and school experiences for an extended period of time are very useful for appraising the growth of retarded children. Standardized test data, as well as data showing evidence of pupil performance can be used to give a well-rounded picture of achievement. As the instructional process proceeds, data should be continually collected. This source of information will enable school personnel to discover other ways of presenting materials as well as providing data about the child and his learning. This process of observing and recording data about student's behavior and progress toward specified objectives can be used to formulate a realistic instructional program.

It is of prime importance that retarded pupils be evaluated in terms of their own abilities and potentialities. The limited mental ability of these pupils does not make it feasible or useful for them to be compared with others in terms of their accomplishments. It seems to be sound educational practice for the present status of each pupil to be compared with his own former achievement in the light of his capabilities, experiences, and temperament. (*See* Appendix E, pp. 136-137)

The teacher should schedule sufficient time in the school day to integrate the observation of each pupil in the plans for class. The evaluation of situations is based upon the knowledge, the abilities, and the limitations of each student. The results do not produce uniformity within any given class. Rather, they account for the diversity of activities, and are as varied as the members of the group and the past experiences they have had.

Plans are made so that goals may be evaluated consistently in terms of:
- understanding, attitudes, skills
- reality of the experience to the individual and the class
- habits changed or found
- initiative, interests, orderly procedure
- responsibility for plans
- participation, cooperation, enjoyment
- self-control, getting along with people
- focus on process as well as product
- work habits
- relationships to home experiences and parents
- interpretation
- needs for changes and modification

Closely related to the general evaluation as stated above are the teacher-pupil evaluations of personal-social competencies as the boys and girls work and play with peers and learn to compete with self, rather than with those around them.*

It is of prime importance that the teacher evaluate the level of understanding and grasp of knowledge which the child has of the materials used. The evaluation can be accomplished during a formal testing period, or informally, by establishing a situation in which the children will have to employ the designated skills without complete awareness that the skill is being tested.†

GOALS AND OBJECTIVES FOR THE RETARDED

Through a systematic approach some evidence should be noted in the changes in performance of the learner, psychologically speaking, if no changes occur as a result of the instructional process, no learning has taken place. Consequently, objectives and goals must be concisely stated if expected behaviors are to be adequately assessed. Administrators and teachers who state goals or objectives in terms of student behavior are showing a more systematic approach to learning, and are in a unique position to judge the efficiency of the teacher-learning process.

Mager's approach to stating and defining behavioral objectives supports the above premise. He stated that:

> "Once an instructor decides he will teach his students something, several kinds of activity are necessary on his part if he is to succeed. He must first decide upon the goals he intends to reach at the end of his course or program. He must then select procedures, content and methods that are relevant to the objectives; cause the student to interact with appropriate subject matter in accordance with principles of learning; and finally, measure or evaluate the student's performance according to the goals or objectives originally selected."**

It should appear that some hierarchy of needs should be evident for retarded children in order to guide them in reaching their optimum growth. A first step for administrators and teachers of retarded children would be to identify goals or objectives.

---

*Baumgertner, *op. cit.,* pp. 45-47.
†Norris G. Haring and Richard L. Schiefelbush, *Methods in Special Education,* (New York: McGraw-Hill, 1967), p. 106.
**Robert Mager, *Preparing Instructional Objectives,* (Palo Alto, California, Fearson Publishers, 1962), Chapter I.

Secondly, to divide them into manageable parts so that the children can succeed. Before sequencing tasks, detailed information should be gathered on each child. Observations appear to be one useful technique for this source. Careful observations will promulgate the status of each child's growth and development. Since all behavior is purposeful, each behavior that the child displays is an effort to meet some need. A good instructional technique is to directly and consciously modify that behavior which is present. Observations will also show the types of environment and conditions in which certain types of behavior are likely or unlikely to occur. Capitalizing on this aspect of child development, goals and objectives will be realistic and relevant.

Consideration of the learning abilities of retardates is another facet that school personnel must carefully consider in establishing goals or objectives. Generally, retarded children have limited attention span; therefore some objectives should be short-termed. Many of the children don't have the ability or patience to labor through long-term objectives. Consequently, retarded children often give up the struggle to master the subject matter. Another point of interest is that goals should emphasize skills and activities that are within the scope of the children's daily lives. It is both psychologically and educationally sound to begin with known experiences and gradually expand these experiences, based upon the abilities of the child. The degree to which goals or objectives are reflected, in academic, social, and personal skills will depend upon the level of retardation and other deficits that the child might have.

PRE-TESTING

Before administrators and teachers can successfully determine if goals or objectives have been accomplished, some prior student input concerning acquired knowledges and skills must be known. The success of any instructional program cannot be fully realized until some initial assessment is made before children begin the instructional process. It is almost impossible to determine whether goals or objectives have been met unless some pre-criterion test has been administered. Pretesting is deemed important for several reasons: (1) to determine if stated objectives are realistic; (2) to guide school personnel in redefining or stating objectives; (3) to give a cross section of abilities and interests in a class; (4) to assist in determining the nature and extent of the program content, including equipment and materials for conducting the program and; (5) to pinpoint the teacher's strengths and weaknesses in the subject.

INSTRUCTIONAL PROCEDURES

As postulated, pretesting will allow administrators to gauge the instructional process, and to sequence learning tasks in a more objective manner. The evaluation of an instructional program should include evidence that the program has or has not reached its objectives, and should also provide the basis for conclusions and recommendations for improving the program. All relevant data should be matched or developed to meet the program's objectives. Data and information not germane to the objectives should not be included in the instructional process.

Recognition by the school of the mentally retarded child as a whole, from the time of his identification to the time of his discharge, would seem to warrant methods of instruction that would take into account all of his general and specific behaviors. These behaviors would include the development of desirable general personality characteristics and the acquisition of specific knowledge and skills that should emanate from the instructional program. In essence, the instructional program should be directly associated with the goals and objectives set forth. Needs, interests, abilities, disabilities, and prior background are also important. These components should be reflected in the objectives and expanded into the instructional program.

The curriculum for the mentally retarded would then be based upon realistic goals and objectives. These objectives in turn should be formulated on the basis of the needs, capacities, and interests of the retarded. School experiences can then be adopted to the limited reasoning power, the meager ability to perceive abstract relationships, and other mental limitations that characterize and handicap the behavior of these pupils.

Individual differences and program scope must be recognized when planning an instructional program for retarded children. Program scope includes the totality of experiences and activities to which an individual is exposed during a specified period of time. Therefore, teachers must be skilled in informal assessment procedures so that both the general and specific characteristics of the children can be described and reacted to in the instructional program. A further criterion of scope is the predicted level of performance each child will be able to attain as an adult. Thus, once the child has been assessed and some prediction made concerning his future capabilities, an instructional program should be tailored to meet his needs. Awareness of the need for sequencing experiences and activities within and between classroom at each level is another important consideration if the educational objectives for these children are to be met.*

By defining goals on a continuum of levels of difficulty, a twofold purpose is accomplished. First, the teacher is assisted in establishing objectives for each class in such a way that they are sequential in an ascending order of difficulty and are also achievable in a foreseeable future. Second, because individual capabilities and competencies vary among children with comparable measurable abilities, such as sequence permits some to move further and faster than others in a single class.

Since most goals for trainable children are essentially short ranged in contrast with the traditional concept of short- and long-range plans for those with more normal intellectual ability, it becomes increasingly important for the stated objectives to be precise and clear cut. In addition, there needs to be frequent evaluation of progress made, together with a review of the estimate of the child's potential in relation to his attainment. Finally, it is important that the limited capacity for growth and learning of the mentally retarded not be dissipated in meaningless or unproductive activity.†

The education of the mentally retarded differs from the education of the average child in the lack of emphasis placed upon

---

*Smith, *Clinical Teaching: Methods of Instruction for the Retarded, op. cit.,* pp. 272-273.
†Haring, *op. cit.,* p. 137.

academic achievement, and the emphasis placed upon the development of personality and adequacy in the occupational and social areas. Mentally handicapped children cannot achieve the skills and degrees of knowledge in the academic areas of reading, writing, arithmetic, science, or social studies attained by the average child. They can, however, learn to adjust to society and to show accomplishment in an unskilled job.*

The key position of the principal in improving the educational program for the mentally retarded requires that he have a basic understanding of the characteristics and needs of these exceptional children and the modification and adaptations required in the total school program. To accomplish this goal, principals must insist that instructional procedures match the program objectives and that tasks are sequenced, based upon the abilities of the children. Thus, the retarded child will be able to achieve and learn without penalty.

EVALUATING PUPIL'S ACHIEVEMENT

Evaluation of pupil's progress should be an on-going process based upon measurable and observable objectives of the instructional program. As indicated, it is of prime importance to assess prior skills before instruction is attempted. After the instructional process, pretest and posttest data should be compared and analyzed to pinpoint changes in the pupil's behavior as a result of instruction. Evaluation will also show possible needed changes in the instructional program. Lack of changes in behavior can be attributed to many factors such as: (1) program content not being relevant to children, (2) lack of materials to implement the program, (3) objectives not being stated in behavioral terms, (4) insufficient time allowed, (5) types of instruments used, (6) tasks not properly sequenced, based upon interest, needs, and abilities of the children, and (7) poor planning and administration to effect change.

A well-planned program will have identified many ways of measuring desired changes and will lend itself to effective

---

*Samuel A. Kirk and G. Orville Johnson, *Educating the Retarded Child*, (Massachusetts: The Riverside Press, 1951), p. 116.

evaluation of retarded children. The following points appear noteworthy of mentioning if administrators are going to assess retardate's achievement in a scientific manner:

1. The objectives must be specified in realistic and relevant terms, which will denote the behavior to be changed.

2. The characteristics, needs, interests, and abilities of the retarded must be identified.

3. The types of measurement to determine whether the objectives of the program were met should be clearly evident.

4. Content of the pre-criterion must match the post-criterion if discrepancies are to be minimized.

5. Some systematic approach should be evident for recording data.

Through the scientific approach, the end product of evaluation should reflect in behavioral changes shown by the students, that is what the student does after the instructional program compared with what he did before he initially entered. Results from this type of evaluation will enable administrators and teachers to objectively evaluate the achievement of retarded children, as well as reflect needed changes or modifications in the program.

A SYSTEM FOR EVALUATING INSTRUCTION

System evaluation (task analysis) has traditionally been associated with trades, and vocational types of programs. Recently, educators have realized the importance of extending this concept to education. Their rationale was predicated upon the principle that identifying tasks and sequencing are two of the chief components of learning. The model below is a simple explanation of how system evaluation can be extended to instruction in the schools.

DESCRIPTION OF SYSTEM EVALUATION

The system is an attempt to visually portray some component parts that should be reflected in sequencing skills and tasks for evaluating achievement of retarded children. Instruction begins with identifying and recording pupil's needs, interests, etc., stating

A SYSTEMATIC MODEL FOR EVALUATING ACHIEVEMENT OF RETARDED CHILDREN*

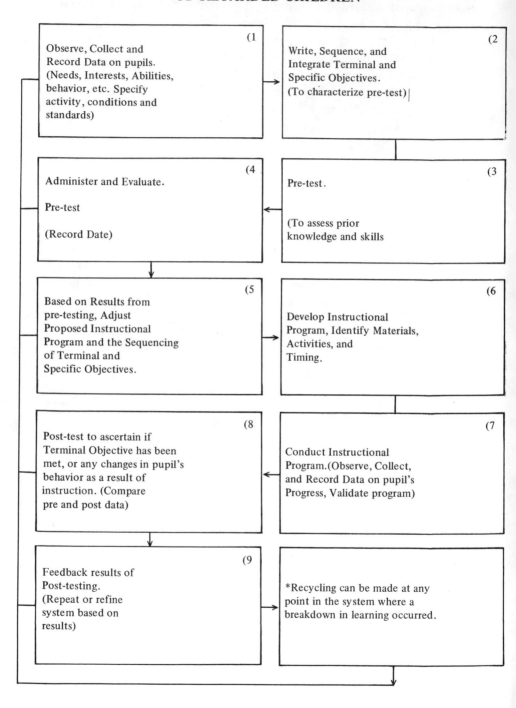

(1 Observe, Collect and Record Data on pupils. (Needs, Interests, Abilities, behavior, etc. Specify activity, conditions and standards)

(2 Write, Sequence, and Integrate Terminal and Specific Objectives. (To characterize pre-test)

(4 Administer and Evaluate. Pre-test (Record Date)

(3 Pre-test. (To assess prior knowledge and skills

(5 Based on Results from pre-testing, Adjust Proposed Instructional Program and the Sequencing of Terminal and Specific Objectives.

(6 Develop Instructional Program, Identify Materials, Activities, and Timing.

(8 Post-test to ascertain if Terminal Objective has been met, or any changes in pupil's behavior as a result of instruction. (Compare pre and post data)

(7 Conduct Instructional Program.(Observe, Collect, and Record Data on pupil's Progress, Validate program)

(9 Feedback results of Post-testing. (Repeat or refine system based on results)

*Recycling can be made at any point in the system where a breakdown in learning occurred.

the activity and conditions under which the program will operate, as well as denoting the minimum standard that will be accepted toward the achievement of the objective. From this point, objectives, testing, and instruction may all be sequenced or broken into tasks. Refining and recycling at any point in the program might be necessary, if expected behavior was not obtained, in light of evaluative data. Negative results might be attributed to tasks not properly sequenced, need for revision in stating objectives, and lack of materials or activities. At any rate, the negative alternatives should be identified before revision in the system is proposed.

Rosenweig* has outlined a list of simple questions to ascertain whether stated objectives have been met for trainable retarded children. They are: (1) the child can do more things for himself; (2) the child is happier than he was; (3) the child is easier to get along with; (4) the child speaks better; (5) the child shows better coordination.

Long- and short-term evaluation requires a definite statement of objectives. Evaluation concerns the extent to which goals have been reached, and can only pose sensible questions when the long- and short-term goals are clearly stated. To be effective evaluation must be a continuous process, and answer two basic questions: (1) are there evidence of pupil's growth, (2) are the experiences received worthwhile for the children?

REPORTING PUPIL'S PROGRESS

Procedures for grading retarded children have generated great concern to parents, children, teachers, and administrators. The chief controversy is whether retarded children should be graded in the same manner as other children. Most retarded children and their parents would rather see a grading system as used in regular classes. Some possible reasons to this approach may be familiarity with the standard grading procedures, to make comparisons of grades with other children in the school and, to use grades to compare achievements of their retarded children with other children with hopes of having their children transferred to regular classes.

---

*Louise Rosenweig, "Report of a School Program for Trainable Mentally Retarded Children," *American Journal of Mental Deficiency, 59,* (Oct., 1954), pp. 181-205.

Administrators generally don't favor standard grading procedures for retardates, chiefly because retardates cannot academically compete with other children. Using the standardized procedures parents will expect their children to receive the same type of diploma as other children. The typical grading procedures permit administrators to issue different diplomas to retarded children, justifying their recommendations on the fact that retarded children have not met the prescribed course of study and are therefore not able to receive a regular diploma.

Finally, teachers become the central figures in grading procedures employed in their schools. They are exposed to pressures from parents, children, and the school's grading policy for retarded children. The teacher becomes a catalyst in the grading controversy attempting to explain the school's grading pattern, and the infeasibility of grading retarded children in the same manner as the normal. Research is desperately needed to shed light on this matter. However, the schools should make sure that parents understand the grading procedures employed and attempt to seek community support concerning their system.*

The type of marks retardates receive deviates from school district to school district, as well as from state to state. The use of marks in evaluating the progress of mentally retarded children is highly questionable. Much of the controversy lies in the fact that administrators in the past had no objective or scientific system to determine the retardate's achievement. The lack of specificity and objectivity of outcomes to be graded and the attitudes of teachers toward pupil interest and effort, reduces decidedly the validity and reliability of marks. The value of a marking system subsequently becomes dependent upon what is being marked, who is doing the marking, who is being marked, and who interprets the marks. Furthermore, marks and accompanying competitive situations can cause many undesirable traits and attitudes to develop in the mentally retarded, such as insecurity, fear, anxiety, cheating, and inferiority. These facts indicate that an objective and scientific way of evaluating the growth of these children should be instituted. Rather than group evaluation, individual evaluation

---

*Smith, *op. cit.*, pp. 272-73.

based upon the unique interest, abilities, disabilities, and characteristics of retardates will aid in their total development. It is recommended that the approach outlined will better provide administrators and teachers with a model that will lead to effective evaluation of the retarded child's achievement.

There is universal agreement that parents should be regularly informed by the school concerning their children's growth and development. The major source of conflict is how should this progress be reported. Administrators should endeavor to explain their grading systems to parents and to seek their support and approval before instituting andy grading pattern on a basis. Teacher/parent conferences appear to be an opportune place to explain and seek parental approval for a marking system.

There are many ways of reporting to parents of retarded children. Some of these ways include report cards, use of descriptive words, check list, narrative or letter reports, conference, pupil self-appraisals, informal notes, telephone conversations, informal meetings, and home visits. It is maintained that as long as parents and school administrators agree upon a marking pattern, and parents understand that their children's achievement is evaluated in relation to their capacities, much of the controversy over marking will be significantly reduced. Reporting can then be viewed as a suitable method of helping parents to accept their handicapped children for what they are, and to understand what the school program is attempting to accomplish, and to learn how well their children are succeeding. Reporting should be a means for strengthening a sound relationship between home and school in the guidance of the child and contribute to the increased effectiveness of learning.* (*See* Appendix D, pp. 134-135)

In conclusion, a systematic approach in evaluating the achievement of retarded children reduces subjectivity, and provides administrators and teachers with an objective model in which to base their appraisal of learning. Evaluation is central to the whole process of determining whether or not an objective has been met. The evaluative process should include not only the

---

*Jackson, Stanley E., "Report Cards: The Marking Problem," *The National Elementary Principal,* 35, (February, 1956), pp. 27-30.

evaluation of students, but also the instructional process. Retarded children should be cognizant of the tasks and activities that are necessary to achieve a stated objective. This will provide some relevancy to the task and facilitate the learning process. Further, it will provide an objective basis for determining achievement and the effects of an instructional program on learning.

CHAPTER 7

WHAT SUPPORTIVE SERVICES
ARE NEEDED?

SPECIAL services should be an integral part of the teaching-learning program for the mentally retarded. Retardation usually denotes many associated problems. Because of these problems, the teacher will find it necessary to call on specialists from other fields for purposes of evaluation and consultation. The school will not be able to provide the comprehensive array of special services required, and therefore, arrangements should be made to use private and community services, in addition to those available within the school system.

Many of the retarded will require medical and paramedical services. The incidence of other types of handicaps is high among this group. Since many of their problems are of a medical nature, the classroom teacher should consult with each child's physician in order to be aware of and know how to handle all possible contingencies. The retarded child from deprived settings will often need to be referred to clinics for a variety of problems since their parents are most often unable to handle their medical needs.*

Adequate community action to meet the total life needs of all those retarded in mental development is dependent, (1) upon the knowledge and competencies of personnel from many disciplines which must be coordinated and utilized, and (2) upon "an expanded program of information and education for the general public and pertinent professional organization."† Agencies providing services for the mentally retarded should be aware of their areas of greatest professional competencies. Implementation of this philosophy will require that all persons think beyond

*Smith, *Clinical Teaching: Methods of Instruction for the Retarded, op. cit.*, p. 271.
†President's Panel on Mental Retardation: Report of the Task Force on Education and Rehabilitation, (U.S. Office of Health, Education, and Welfare, 1962), p. 57.

traditional approaches of individual agencies as they now exist. Program levels could be raised if special services were obtained from agencies best equipped to provide them. Barriers which make general community services unavailable to the mentally retarded should be removed. The retarded should have access to all services which are applicable to his needs. Enriched or special services should be provided so that each retarded person may develop to his fullest potential. Mental retardation must not be seen as a single symptom, but as a host of disabilities in the physical, psychological, and social areas. Because of the complexity of the problem, services should encompass a variety of professional disciplines. No single profession can meet the many needs of the retarded. The professional team should function initially as a diagnostic team, incorporating the findings of other team members in their decision process. If at all possible, the initial team should participate in the treatment and follow-up process.

Diagnostic evaluation, if broadly perceived, can play an important role in the management of handicapping conditions in childhood. Beck* pointed out if the diagnostic study is carried out by experts and specialists from various disciplines, the need for repetition of full study on referrals can be achieved more easily. Allen and Lelchuck† indicated that the staff of the diagnostic clinic has at its disposal the information that was obtained in the intake procedures as well as the information that has been requested from other hospitals and physicians. The social worker assigned to the patient usually accompanies him during the history-taking session. During the physical examination, it is often possible for the social worker to develop further rapport with the family. The clinical psychologists may be introduced to the family by the social worker. A conference is held between the staff members. Plans are made for needed studies and preliminary impressions are recorded. Specialized studies, such as formal psychological, medical, and orthopedic evaluations, are scheduled

---

*Helen Beck, "The Advantages of a Multipurpose Clinic for the Mentally Retarded," *American Journal of Mental Deficiency, 66*(5), (March, 1962), pp. 789-94.
†John Allen and Louis Lelchuck, "A Comprehensive Care Program for Children with Handicaps," *Journal of Disease of Children, 3,* (March, 1966), pp. 229-35.

when indicated.*

A diagnostic evaluation according to Drayer† and Stafford** almost always includes a thorough review of development, social functioning, a specific history of the presenting problems, psychiatric, pediatric, neurological, and psychological examinations. A clinic should also maintain or have access to facilities for laboratory examinations, speech and hearing evaluations. Grant†† implied that the public health nurse can yield valuable information regarding the child's development, general physical health, interests, abilities, and relationships within and outside the family. Her observations frequently make it possible to assess parental reaction to the child, the level of family anxiety and the ability of the family to carry out home training regiments. Levinson¶ stated that the making of a diagnostic and planning of a guidance program for retarded children takes the combined efforts of many specialists.

Supervisors of special education and vocational and/or regular counselors should also comprise the evaluation team. The supervisor should work closely with the principal in coordinating the efforts of all those who act as resource personnel for the teacher of retarded children. With the guidance of the principal and supervisor, the teacher is made more keenly aware of the factors which contribute to the growth and development of the mentally retarded. The other specialists give help to the teacher by cooperatively interpreting and analyzing pupil problems and by giving assistance in developing plans and activities for meeting the needs of each pupil. Joint participation of teacher and specialists in meeting pupil problems enables research and current findings in the field of mental retardation to become a part of daily classroom teaching. Teamwork of teacher and specialists can be of major

*A. B. Silverstein, "Psychological Testing Practices in State Institutions for the Mentally Retarded," *The American Journal of Mental Deficiency, 68*(3), (November, 1963), pp. 440-45.

†Carl Drayer and Elfriede Schesinger, "The Informing Interview," *The American Journal Journal of Mental Deficiency, 65,* (Nov., 1960), pp. 363-70.

**Richard Stafford and Robert J. Meyer, *op. cit.,* p. 151-55.

††Dorothy Grant, *et. al.,* "A Program for Mentally Retarded Children in a Child Health Clinic Setting," (Washington, D.C., Bureau of Maternal and Child Care, 1966).

¶ Abraham Levinson, *The Mentally Retarded Child.* (New York, John Day Co., 1965).

assistance to the teacher in doing a better job in meeting the needs of the retarded.

AN INTEGRATED APPROACH TO MEETING NEEDS

The integrated approach to learning which is so necessary for the mentally retarded requires that the services of specialists be coordinated and integrated with the work of the teacher. A teacher of handicapped pupils is likely to find many handicaps and maladjustments, such as speech disorders, defective hearing, poor reading ability, weak eyesight, motor disabilities, and behavioral maladjustments are but a few of the existing difficulties. The problems of mental retardation are so intricate and extensive that many specialists will be needed in the evaluation and treatment process. Specialists in various disciplines should be consulted as the needs of the retarded child dictates.

Since variations in the severity of mental handicaps come about as a result of the complex interaction of biological and environmental influences, Kelman* informs us that the determination of the degree of mental handicap is a complex problem and cannot be qualified adequately on the basis of a mere test score. It must include a careful estimate of the medical aspects of the condition; a thorough estimate of the whole child; his social experiences; his family life; schooling; and the social contacts; and must weigh the effects of other complicating factors such as speech disabilities or sensory and motor defects. The goals of treatment should be individual and realistic. Some will require short-term and some long-term planning. Such goals should be based upon careful evaluation of the child's handicap as well as his assets and capacities. One of the major purposes of integrated services should be to improve the identification process of children with developmental problems.

The mentally retarded should be identified as early in their school life as possible by qualified experts. Early identification of the mentally retarded is necessary if the school is to give maximum help. Without early identification, there is the danger

---

*Howard Kelman, "The Function of a Clinic for Mentally Retarded Children," *Social Case Work,* May, 1956.

that many mentally retarded children will be expected to fulfill unreasonable demands and expectations. Their inability to cope with situations beyond their capacities can lead to fear, anxiety and maladjustment. When their handicap is not known, they are likely to be misunderstood and misdirected as they attempt to meet their needs. Their behavior becomes upset and later tasks of helping them make better psychological and social adjustments become more difficult.

It would be helpful to everyone concerned if these children were identified during their preschool years. Despite the difficulty of diagnosing mental handicaps in very young children of preschool age, early identification is possible. Mentally deficient children of preschool age can first be located through referrals by parents, pediatricians, public health organizations, and social agencies. They can then be referred to psychological clinics for diagnosis. Early identification can be made by careful and thorough case study which includes the use of mental tests suitable for very young children. When these children enter school with their handicap already diagnosed, the school can better meet their needs from the beginning of their school life. The possibilities of failure, anxiety, frustration, and rejection in their experience will thereby be reduced.

Accurate identification of the mentally retarded, whether before or after entering school, depends upon thorough, complete clinical procedures. There cannot be complete reliance upon observation and subjective judgment alone. Symptoms of mental retardation may be false and misleading. Passivity, aggressive, antisocial behavior, lack of reading ability, poor health, low marks, and defective articulation do not necessarily indicate subnormal mental development. These symptoms may be the result of negative personal or environmental factors apart from subnormal intelligence. Children identified as mentally retarded on a subjective basis alone may thus be done a grave injustice.

SPEECH DEFECTS

Research supports the above premise concerning misleading

symptoms of mental retardation. Sheenan and others* conducted a survey of speech disorders in state institutions for the retarded in California (IQ 25-39). They found mentally retarded patients' stuttering to be about the same as that of the normal population. Over 216 subjects were included in the sample; of this number over half had either speech defects or severely delayed speech. Dental abnormalities and articulation disorders were common. Only 12% of the subjects examined had speech that could be considered normal. Three voice problems, two aphasic patients, one stutterer, and one clutter made up the remainder of speech disorders found in the group. They concluded that the ratio of stutterers among the retarded doesn't differ significantly from the normal population. Findings by Goertzen† reported two studies of institutionalized mentally retarded children. We found the following percentages of patients with speech defects or no speech at all in three common subdivisions of the retarded level:

Table I

Intellectual Level	(Kennedy) % Speech Defects	(Sirkin, Jacob & Lyons) % Speech Defects
Educable M. R.	42.6	43.0
Severely M. R.	96.9	74.0
Total — Care M. R.	100.0	100.0

American Journal of Mental Deficiency, 1957, 62, pp. 244-253. Reprinted by permission of the author and the publisher.

Lubman's study** was concerned with a speech program for severely retarded children in parent-operated classes in Cleveland, Ohio. He found only 7 of 150 children did not need speech therapy. Research consistently shows that when retarded pupils are compared with normal children there is a higher incidence of speech defects among the retarded.

*Joseph Sheenan, Margaret Martyn, and Kent L. Kilburn, "Speech Disorders in Retardation," *The American Journal of Mental Deficiency, 73*(2), (Sept., 1968), pp. 251-56.
†Stanley M. Goertzen, "Speech and the Mentally Retarded Child," *The American Journal of Mental Deficiency, 62,* (Sept., 1957), pp. 244-53.
**C. G. Lubman, "Speech Program for Severely Retarded Children," *The American Journal of Mental Deficiency, 60,* (Oct., 1955), pp. 297-300.

VISUAL DEFECTS

The Frostig Developmental Test of Visual Perception was administered to 148 retarded children. Mean age was fourteen years, the average subjects scores were at above the same level as those of the average five-year-old child in the standardized sample. The correlations of the subjects with both age and IQ were positive and, for the most part, highly significant.* Paraskeva† made a survey of twenty-nine residential schools for the blind in the United States. Findings revealed that approximately 15 percent of the blind students were also mentally retarded. Findings by Long and Perry** were essentially the same. The American Printing House for the Blind†† conducted a survey of multiple disabilities among children in residential schools and day classes for the visually impaired. Nineteen and six-tenths percent of the subjects had one or more handicapping conditions other than blindness. Residential school programs had fewer multiple handicapped children than day school programs. Mental retardation was found in 7.9 percent of the blind children. DiMichael¶ states that 10 to 14 percent of blind children between the ages of five and seventeen are retarded. He questioned the validity of using standardized IQ tests for the retarded-blind. His basic concern was whether the IQ and M.A. guides, derived from IQ tests, given for the educable and trainable should apply to individuals with multiple handicaps.

HEARING IMPAIRED

Harlow§ clearly pointed out the need for adequate hearing tests

*A. B. Silverstein, Virginia Unfeldt, and Edette Price, "Clinical Assessment of Visual Perceptual Abilities in the Mentally Retarded," *American Journal of Mental Deficiency,* 74(4), (January, 1970), pp. 524-26.

†Peter C. Paraskeva, "A Survey of the Facilities for the Mentally Retarded-Blind in the United States," *The International Journal for the Blind, 8,* (May, 1959), pp. 139-45.

**J. Perry and Elinor Long, "Slow Learner and Retarded Blind Child," (43rd Biennal Convention, American Assoc. of Instructors for the Blind, 1956).

††American Printing House for the Blind Report, "The survey of the Multiple-Handicapped, Visual Handicapped," (Louisville, Kentucky, 1955).

¶Salvador DiMichael G., "Meeting the Needs of Retarded Blind Children," (43rd Biennial Convention, American Assoc. of Instructors of the Blind, 1956).

§Joyce L. Harlow, "Mentally Retarded or Hearing Impaired," *The Volta Review, 69,* (Dec., 1967), pp. 664-67.

for students labeled as mentally retarded. He stated cases where students have been mistakenly diagnosed as mentally retarded but when further diagnosed, it was revealed that their hearing was severely impaired. When fitted with hearing aids, many so called retarded individuals showed more intellectual potential than at first suspected. Due to the lateness of identifying the hearing loss, Harlow indicated that it was necessary to place students in classes for the deaf so that they receive special education training for the hard of hearing children. Generally, behavior improved when children were properly placed in an educational setting. Rittmanic* and Schlanger† audiometric studies of school aged children in institutions for the mentally retarded showed that between 17 and 19.8 percent of the population studied were found to have significant hearing loss, where that term was defined at 15db loss or greater in two or more frequencies. The Johnston and Farrell** study supported the above. They stated that hearing loss in five times the incidence that would be expected from a similar survey among public school children. Investigations by Siegenthaler and Kryzwicki,†† Johnson and Farrell¶ pinpointed a higher incidence of hearing impairment and disability in retarded children. It would appear that the lower the intelligence index, the greater the incidence of hearing defects would occur. The authors estimated that between 13 to 49 percent of retarded children have hearing impairment depending upon the criteria employed. A conservative estimation for the general school population with hearing impairment range from 3 to 10 percent.

---

*Paul A. Rittmanic, "Hearing Rehabilitation for the Institutionalized Mentally Retarded," *American Journal of Mental Deficiency, 63,* (March, 1959), pp. 778-83.

†B. B. Schlanger and R. H. Gottsleben, "Clinical Speech Program at the Training School at Vineland," *American Journal of Mental Deficiency, 61,* (Jan., 1957), pp. 516-21.

**P. W. Johnston and M. J. Farrel, "An Experiment in Improving Medical and Educational Services for Hard of Hearing Children at the Walter Fernald State School," *American Journal of Mental Deficiency, 62,* (Nov., 1957), pp. 230-37.

††R. M. Siegenthaler and D. F. Kryzwicki, "Incidence and Patterns of Hearing Loss Among an Adult Mentally Retarded Population," *American Journal of Mental Deficiency, 64,* (Nov., 1959), pp. 444-49.

¶P. W. Johnston and M. J. Farrell, "Auditory Impairments Among Resident School Children at the Walter E. Fernald State School," *American Journal of Mental Deficiency, 58,* (April, 1954), pp. 640-44.

The cited research is by no means comprehensive enough to represent the preponderance of studies dealing with multiple handicaps among retarded children. The rationale was to promulgate the notion that generally retarded children have a higher incidence of defects other than retardation when compared to the normal population. Another reason for the cited studies was to reflect the intricacies of assessing retardates with multiple handicapping conditions. When reviewing studies dealing with retarded children with multiple handicaps, a few have clearly demonstrated that a small percentage of them compare with children in their age groups. The implications for school administrators is not to assume because the child is retarded that he will have other defects in the physical, social, and sensory areas, rather to make sure that he is properly assessed by qualified personnel and a school program initiated based upon his abilities, needs, and interests.

There is a need for improved instruments to assess retarded children with multiple handicaps, more research is needed concerning their learning potentialities, a consensus on terms and classifications will greatly enhance the identification process, and a system developed where as information concerning learning, habits, traits, skills, and instructional procedures can filter directly into the schools to aid in developing an instructional program.

From the aforementioned research it becomes quite clear that many of the problems of retarded children are too complex for the teacher to solve alone; he needs the services of many specialists to assist him in promoting better pupil growth and adjustment. Any information received by the teacher concerning retarded children can facilitate his instructional process. The school psychologist appears to be in a unique position to assist the teacher in developing a detailed profile concerning the child's behavior. Teachers can do much to assist the psychologist by clearly spelling out the purpose of the referral followed by questions he wants answered.*

It is essential that objective procedures be used in conjunction with observations and subjective judgment for identifying the

*Frederic B. Nalven, "How Can Psychological Test Reports Be Used by Teachers of Educable Mentally Retarded Children," *Education and Training of the Mentally Retarded,* 4(3), (October, 1969), pp. 113-18.

mentally retarded. Qualified experts, who have a basic under-standing of mental deficiency and its implications for education, should administer the necessary objective measures. Their diagnosis would include more than the use of intelligence tests. The child is studied as a whole. The health, social competency, personality and home background of each pupil are among the factors that are objectively studied. A complete identification procedure could involve many specialists including psychologists, psychiatrists, social workers, physicians, nurses and clinicians. The services of many, if not all, of these persons are desired in order that all factors affecting intellectual response may be accurately known and a complete and accurate picture of the child as a whole may be obtained. The efforts of these experts will, of course, be aided by the cooperation of teachers, parents, and administrators.

A plan of action by the school for identifying the mentally retarded may include the following seven procedures:

1. The use of an effective screening method that is in accord with these recommendations:

   a. It should be reasonably objective.
   b. It should not require knowledge and skills beyond one's professional training (e.g. selection and administration of group intelligence tests by teachers who may be in-adequately trained to do so; teacher's evaluation of a child as being mentally handicapped).
   c. It should be easily administered.
   d. It should reach all pupils.
   e. It should consider the child's actual performance in school.
   f. It should have a high degree of accuracy, i.e. better than 50 percent of the children referred to the psychologist should be mentally handicapped.*

Screening techniques, to be thorough, would include these courses of action:

   a. Data are collected from each teacher on a form that lists the name, age, and reading, arithmetic, spelling grade levels of each child. Teachers of kindergarten and first grade report

---

*Isaac Jolles, "Discovering the Educable Mentally Handicapped: A Public Schooling Screening Technique," *American Journal of Mental Deficiency, 56,* (April, 1955), pp. 610-16.

the social maturity of each child. These data are turned over to a psychologist for interpretation. This interpretation is based upon these hypotheses:

1. An educable mentally handicapped child does not begin to do beginning first grade work in any subject until developmentally he is ready for such tasks.
2. Once an educable mentally handicapped child begins to learn academic work, he progresses (in regular classes) about one-half year to every full year for the normal child.
3. A mentally handicapped child who is not yet eight years old is not likely to be socially mature enough for first grade, and five or six year-olds who are socially mature enough for kindergarten is not likely to be mentally handicapped.

After these data have been checked to determine which children cannot succeed in regular classes, even with supportive help for the teacher, a frequency distribution table is constructed showing the number of potential candidates for special class placement in each age group. On the basis of the total number of potential special class pupils, availability of classrooms and trained teachers, a conclusion is reached concerning how many special classes are to be established.

b. Further elimination is made when a large number of potentially mentally handicapped children indicate the need for the special placement and there are questions involved concerning the accuracy of the survey data. In these instances children under the age of nine are given an intelligence test in small groups. Older children may be tested also and given reading and arithmetic tests in addition to the intelligence test. If either the intelligence test or achievement test indicates that the pupil is not mentally handicapped, that child is eliminated as a potential candidate.

c. The final step is the filling out of the Referral for Psychological Services form by the classroom teacher. These items from the referral form appear to be significant: birthplace of parents, father's occupation, special abilities, school history, report card grades, personality and behavior traits. No single item is considered as sufficient reason for rejecting a child as being a potential mentally handicapped child.*

An effective screening method for referral seems necessary in order to save time and money and to reduce the load of psychological services. Lack of money and personnel, with demands for services exceeding both, does not seem to be a rare occurrence for psychological services in a large school system.

2. Prompt referral for individual psychological examination is made when the need is determined. The major responsibility for submitting and speeding up referrals usually lies with the principal. His strategic position of leadership can be a factor in determining how soon requests for examination of pupils are made. Referrals for examination usually come from the principal and teacher, but it is possible that parents, the school psychologists, doctor, nurse, or a special referral official may take the initiative.

A referral blank form that is used when a child is recommended for examination includes as much pertinent information about the child as is readily available. This information will assist the diagnosticians in making an accurate appraisal of the child's handicap. The referral form includes general factual information about the child, together with a detailed statement giving specific reasons for submission of the referral. Additional helpful information to be submitted might include the child's school history, progress, physical condition, latest achievement, and intelligence test results when available, personality and adjustment, home and community conditions, and family history and cooperation.

3. As a first step in the examination following the referral, the child is given a complete psychological examination. This examination may include a group intelligence test for further screening purposes, to be followed by individual verbal and performance tests. The intelligence tests may be supplemented by tests that indicate personality and social needs of the child, particularly when there is the possibility that these factors may have affected his test performance adversely.

4. A medical examination is important for determining defects

---

*Ibid.

in hearing, eyesight, mental health and general all-around physical condition. Mental retardation may have a constitutional cause that can be treated. In selected cases, comprehensive psychiatric examination may be warranted.

5. In obtaining a complete picture of the child, an individual achievement evaluation is important for determining educational disabilities. This evaluation can be based on individual placement diagnostic and aptitude data.

6. A study of the child's background history of a family and community is important in order that possible causative factors in those areas can be determined.

7. The identification of a child as mentally retarded is not reached until the comprehensive case studies have been completed and all major influences upon the child's behavior have been carefully and thoroughly studied by skilled diagnosticians.

Once the team's findings have been submitted to the school, the teacher can outline the psycho-social strengths and weaknesses of the skills and take appropriate action for instruction. If the findings indicate motor disabilities, the teacher can use this information with the aid of specialists to determine whether or not this disability affects the child's academic skills. Finally, the diagnostic report should give a prognostic view of the child's abilities and disabilities. This will enable the teacher to program for immediate and long-range needs.

A principal can do much to facilitate and unify the efforts of teachers and service specialists in identifying, diagnosing, treating, and preventing problems of pupils' difficulties and aberrations. The principal can plan coopera-tively with teachers and specialists, procedures that will enable everyone to work together as a team in seeking the underlying causes of adjustment problems and in developing a remedial and preventive program. He is in the best position to outline the philosophy of the school as it is applied to the retarded. In addition, principals should advance the concept that a child is not necessarily per-manently and irrevocably labeled as mentally retarded once he has been diagnosed as such. A prompt re-examination is to occur whenever there is doubt concerning accuracy of the identification. Influences of all factors affecting intellectual response should then be carefully reconsidered.

COORDINATION OF ACTIVITIES

Coordination of the education program for the mentally retarded should exist among and between all units of the school system and community. Effective planning for the mentally retarded calls for participation of many agencies, official and voluntary, local and regional. In order for the retardate to receive maximum benefit from community programs, there needs to be closely coordinated activities with the schools. Until the turn of the last one or two decades, the responsibility for preparing the retarded youth to assume the obligations of a mature citizen was almost exclusively that of the school. Presently certain social and vocational services external to the school which had as their purpose the rendering of training, and placement services to handicapped persons of postschool age begin to assist the schools in these attempts. These agencies developed separately from the school and remained at some distance until recently when they and the schools recognized a mutuality of interests and purposes. Today, the nature of the interaction between schools and other community agencies is of such a nature that there has come to be a depending of one on the other to so accomplish its mission that a continuity and harmony between them to be effected. The responsibility for educating the mentally retarded does not rest with the elementary school alone. All levels of the public school system and community are responsible for educating all the children of all the people.

Regular and continuous progress of the mentally retarded through the school system requires coordination of effort on the part of community, administrators, and teachers. The elementary and secondary schools need to be unified in purpose and procedure so that steady, continuous progress of the retarded may be insured. Despite an increase in coordination between levels of education in the public schools and a commitment to team efforts, school personnel still place too much emphasis on how to use the findings of other professionals rather than how to work with the team to establish and improve a quality program for retarded children. The team concept needs a prominent place in the school's organizational pattern that will uncover the importance of relating to other professionals. How effectively the team will operate by group decisions and carefully sifted evidence will also depend to a great extent upon the administrator's confidence in himself and the faculty. His ability to weave properly into the daily schedule all the diverse elements of medical treatment, therapies, testing, guidance, and special teaching, as well as social and recreational activities, needed by individual retarded children will test the comprehensiveness of a successful school program.

Diagnostic information can be used by the schools to design effective programs tailored to the needs and interests of the retarded child. Evaluation findings also pinpoint modifications needed in the school curricula so that the child can benefit from educational experiences. The school can plan for trained personnel, supplies, equipment, and special services based on the assessment. Teachers must employ methods and materials suited to the individual's unique pattern of needs, interests, abilities, and motivation. Properly used, this information can provide the teacher with a vehicle for individualized instruction and provide some avenue for the child to succeed in his educational pursuits. A first step in making diagnostic information relevant to the schools is the retrieval of accurate, descriptive data that can be used in the instructional process.

Meyer* advocated that community groups should join together to plan for children with handicapping conditions. This plan should be a joint effort combining all aspects and professionals in the community. Community organizations can greatly facilitate services to the handicapped child. Effective diagnosis should be interdisciplinary in nature and should point the way to adequate treatment and evaluation. Parents are a prime concern in community planning and should be involved throughout the total process if the treatment is to be beneficial to the child. Properly instituted, community planning can greatly aid the child with developmental and/or learning disorders.

*Roger Meyer, "Community Planning for Children with Developmental and Learning Disorders," *The Journal of School Health, 38*(4), (April, 1968), pp. 246-7.

Communities can do a great deal to make better use of their resources through a coordination of efforts. Coordination mobilizes the skills of people to help all programs, eliminates wasteful competition, saves money, improves training opportunities, and gives invaluable assistance to the retarded child and his family. The school should be the key for coordinating activities in the community. Specialists in various disciplines should be consulted as the need of the retarded child dictates. Some consideration should be given to the parents who may need financial assistance. Again, personnel in diagnostic centers can refer the parent to appropriate community agencies who can provide the support.

Differentiation of general and specialized services is vital, not only to make ample use of community resources but to provide the retarded child with a complete diagnosis. Since services provide for the retarded child should include both approaches. Coordinated planning should be a well planned process that seeks to elicit cooperation and communication among various community agencies. Some of the problems associated with effective community planning are: (1) lack of personnel with experience to conduct the planning, (2) decreased interdisciplinary communication due to lack of mutual respect among specialists, (3) facilities for the retarded failing to recognize that no one clinic or agency can provide the necessary services needed to diagnose, treat, and rehabilitate the retarded child, and (4) exclusion of parents from the initial diagnostic evaluation, treatment, and follow-up procedures.

The position of the school personnel on a special education team headed by noneducators and the relationship of medical personnel with other members are some specific problems that should not vary as widely as they do from program to program. Understanding the intricacies of teamwork and agreement upon its definition might clarify areas of misunderstanding. The necessity of communication within the team, of team action with parents, community members, state departments, and other programs, as well as balancing progress, morals, and democratic ideals constitute other areas of coordination sometimes overlooked by administrators.*

MULTIDISCIPLINARY APPROACH NEEDED

The problem of multidisciplinary communication can become a handicap in providing comprehensive care for the retarded in several ways:

1. Terminology. Various disciplines applied different terms to the mentally handicapped which might denote a different meaning to the individual specialist. Some unanimity of terms among the professionals would do much to expedite services for the retarded.

2. Roles of the specialists. Mental retardation must be seen as a problem with many psychological, physical, and social factors. These problems should be attacked by various specialists in their prospective fields, with no one problem being paramount or taking precedence over the others, only in unique situations.

3. Classifications. Many classification systems are based upon etiology factors, behavioral characteristics of the child, and intelligence test results. There is a lack of consonance among specialists in this area. It would appear that the American Association on Mental Deficiency is defensible. According to the review scheme of classification, an individual may not be termed mentally retarded unless he is deficient in measured intelligence and adaptive behavior.†

When some common consensus of terms and etiological factors have been realized, the team's findings can be incorporated into the school's plan for educating the retarded child. The school must include other agencies in the community for the education and treatment of retarded pupils. Cooperation between the school and agencies in the community is essential if the needs of the retardates are to be effectively met. Coordination of service also avoids duplication of efforts to service retardates in the community.

---

*Leo E. Connor, *Administration of Special Education Programs,* (New York, Columbia University Press, 1961), p. 111.

†Heber, "Manual on Terminology and Classification in Mental Retardation," *op. cit.,* p. 98.

COMPREHENSIVE SERVICES FOR THE RETARDED

Methods must be developed to provide for more effective use of other personnel concerned with the mentally retarded. It was reported in the President's Task Force* that many of the duties performed by specialists in various fields should be done by nonprofessionals under their directions, thus relieving them for additional time to relate to tasks for which they have been trained. Many of the needs of the retarded are similar to the general population, the basic difference is that many specialized services are required because of the complexity and wide range of handicapping conditions that exist among the group. Therefore, specialists should be freed from routine duties, and engage in the specified discipline in which they were trained.

For purposes of achieving comprehensive services for exceptional children, schools should be prepared to go beyond their traditional role as coordinators or users of other community services. Schools should provide leadership in developing new and experimental forms of comprehensive child and family services, perhaps through broad new regional agencies. For children with special needs the school might implement and provide direct child health clinics, special diagnostic and therapeutic programs, as well as welfare services designed to provide for the physical and material needs of the child. Vocational guidance, counseling, and rehabilitative services should be consolidated to provide more effective services. Instructional programs for children with highly special needs should be centrally located, with boarding and residential facilities provided by the school system for children from isolated rural areas. Homebound and hospital instruction would be provided for children not able to attend school. Nursery school and early education programs in the home would be provided for children as integral parts of the total educational system. Schools should be responsible for reducing the "drop-out" problem by reflecting the interests and needs of children with cultural backgrounds and educational needs that differ from the larger segments of society.

---

*President's Panel on Mental Retardation, *op. cit.*, p. 70.

These concerns for providing coordinated services for handi-capped children have created some controversy for the role of the school in providing this type of service. Some authorities would limit the schools in this area, others maintain that many handicapped children and their families are not properly served because of the fragmentation of responsibilities for services among many agencies and professions, frequently it is difficult to achieve coordinated child-centered and family-centered services. No clear answers to this conflict is evident, but research and innovations should be attempted to find solutions.*

Mutual school and community understanding and support is needed in providing the mentally retarded with the best educational program possible. Educators are giving increasing attention to the interpretation of educational programs to the public. They realize that the schools belong to the people of the community and that education is a matter of public concern. Education is costly and those who foot the bill have the right to know how their monies are being expended and what they are receiving for their tax dollars.†

It is commonly agreed that a desirable relationship between school and community is one that is marked by a strong bond of understanding and cooperation. Parents should have a share in developing the aims and purposes of the program which the school is providing. Parents should be welcome, helpful partners in the school in the guidance of the retarded child.

It is of prime importance that administrators devise ways and methods for informing the public. They should utilize many techniques in telling the story of education to the citizens of the community. Reports to parents, adult use of school resources, school utilization of community agencies and organizations, and parent-teacher groups are some of the major avenues of interaction that can exist between the school and the immediate community. Through these channels the school can interpret and proliferate its programs to the community and can enlist the cooperation of the

---

*Policy Statements: Call for Response, "Basic Commitments and Responsibilities to Exceptional Children," *Exceptional Children, 37*(6), (Feb., 1971), 426-427.

†William M. Cruickshank and G. Orvile Johnson, Eds., *Education of Exceptional Children and Youth,* (New Jersey, Prentice-Hall, 1967), p. 697.

community in the maintenance and improvement of the policies.

Rusalem* enumerated that administrators of special education programs do not always utilize their activities as a part of a continuing problem. Time and effort spent in community and coordinating with other agencies seem to be of little immediate value to the retarded child, only vigorous espousal of the idea that special education has a responsibility to join with any accommodating team or agency will insure a brighter future for retarded children.

Baumgartner† voiced that each community must be prepared in its thinking, its desire, and in its understanding to accept the mentally retarded as useful citizens. The basic facts placed before the public can lead to communication and intelligent action. Only as the administrator and the supervisor assume constructive leadership in special education, as it relates to other community services and strength, can there be a complete program. Then the community program will reflect the belief and the understanding of the principal and other school administrators. The principal should assume the leadership in bringing the school and community closer together. It is he who carries the major responsibility for helping to develop healthy school-community relations. As the public becomes aware of the objectives and work of the school, the public will have a chance to develop positive attitudes towards the children and offer its cooperation in working with the school.

Full interaction between school and community can bring many resource personnel into the school and the classroom. Workers and artists of the community can come into the life of the retarded children to bring a wider knowledge of the world, its occupation, and its finer pleasures. School-community interaction brings parents into the classroom to see their children at work and at play. Better understanding of what the school is trying to accomplish can result in parents being better able to share in promoting the objectives of the school.

Community agencies such as health clinics, child adjustment

---

*H. Rusalem, "Special Teacher on the Interdisciplinary Team," *Exceptional Children*, *26*, (December, 1959), pp. 180-81.
†Baumgartner, *op. cit.*, p. 149.

centers and others can join with parents and school personnel in promoting the growth of the retarded. The needs of most retarded children are so vast and require extensive service in several areas, because of this need the schools will have to depend heavily upon community agencies to meet the many needs of retarded children or to implement services within its own structure. As Fischer* so wisely stated, the school has many functions to perform: for the child, for the family, for the community, and for the nation. Its mission should not be made to appear simpler or narrower than it properly is. But neither should it be expected to assume responsibilities that belong more appropriately to other agencies. The wisest course toward a sound community establishment of services lies in the direction of joint effort. When all agencies combine to define their respective functions and simultaneously to build a network of relationships so that they may communicate and cooperate, the results are certain to be good. The most effective way to integrate services is through local leadership. This is the most effective way to concentrate the available resources upon the problems of raising to the highest level the quality of services provided to meet local needs.

Sheltered workshops, places of employment for handicapped persons who require a type of close job supervision not available in normal private industry, are valuable assets to some communities. They offer a protective environment for the mentally retarded, who, as potential wage earners, are not easily adjusted to the outside industrial world without assistance. The jobs in the workshop are sublet from industry and are geared to the skills of the retarded. All of the community services mentioned can offer specialized help to the mentally retarded and their parents in solving the diverse problems of adjustment, health, employment, and education. Sheltered workshops must be flexible in order to adjust to changes in the community and labor conditions. Training programs will be of little use to retardates if they are so limited or sheltered that they fail to provide realistic work experiences, or if

*John H. Fischer, "The Community and Its Schools: The Community's Responsibilities," *Children, 11,* (January, 1964), pp. 3-12.

they fail to train individuals for the type of work experiences they will encounter on the job. Both the physical and social factors of the community must be assessed so that training will not be an exercise in futility.

PARENTAL INVOLVEMENT

The importance of including parents in the total educational sphere of their children has been reflected to some degree throughout this chapter.* This section will deal generally with how the schools can elicit and involve parents in the educational process, as well as some problems encountered by parents of retarded children.

Presently, there has been an increase in the interest of the mentally retarded and his personal welfare. In past decades the emphasis was mainly on the social consequences of developmental deficiencies. Currently, efforts are being made to assist the child *and* his family. It is commonly recognized that no program will be completed successfully unless some parental involvement is sought and maintained. Cooperation between parents and school can aid the child greatly in his educational pursuits. Professional workers generally recognize that most parents have difficulty in accepting and adjusting to their retarded children. Consequently, without proper guidance these factors can hamper the progress of the retarded child.

A first step for parents in accepting their children's retardation is to recognize the basic problem, and to seek ways to face the problems or retardation with a positive approach. The difficulty of the problem is immense for most parents. Many will need individualized as well as group counseling. As mentioned, the school can provide some counseling for parents if their problems are not too deep-rooted. More severe problems will have to be attended to by mental health specialists. The salient point that school officials should keep centrally in mind is that some parents have received counseling and are ready to assist in educating their children, others are not so fortunate. Astute administrators may

---

*See Chapter 8 for further discussion and references.

be able to distinguish between the two groups and take appropriate action for the welfare of the child.

Administrators can employ many techniques to assist and involve parents in the educational process. Some of the commonly known techniques are workshops, parent-teacher conferences, and parent study groups. These approaches, other than parent-teacher conferences, are generally group based, parents who have common problems can discuss them as well as experts from various disciplines can address the group. The principal sets the stage for parental involvement by working with school and community personnel. Joint planning and involvement between the school and parents cannot but help boost the parents' self-concept by incorporating them in the educational process.

As a means of strengthening the family in fulfilling its obligations to children who have exceptional needs, the schools should provide educationally related counseling and family services. In cases of clear educational neglect, the schools, through qualified professional personnel, should make extraordinary arrangements for preventive and compensatory educational services. As a means of strengthening special education programs, parents of handicapped children and organized community groups should be given a responsible part in educational policy formation and planning activities.*

As outlined, assistance to parents is important in helping them resolve social and emotional difficulties affecting the child and to give advice regarding a plan for care of their children as well as decisions concerning treatment and educational placement to ameliorate the handicapping condition. Diagnostic evaluation should further assist parents in accepting the fact that their child is retarded and to provide information that will assist them in meeting the day to day problems that will arise. If the child is trainable, concrete directions should be given to assist the child in achieving self-help skills and other nonacademic skills within his capacity. For the educable retarded, the evaluation should point to specific guidance that should be given the child so that he might reach his optimum growth.

---

*Policy Statements: Call for Response, "Exceptional Children," 1971, *op. cit.*, p. 427.

If made available, diagnostic evaluation carefully interpretated can do much to dispel the ill advice given to parents by friends concerning mental deficiency and point the way to effective treatment of the retarded child. In addition these findings will greatly assist the parent in his emotional conflicts concerning his retarded child by relieving anxieties, frustrations, and conflicts which impede the emotional development of both parent and child.

COUNSELING AND GUIDANCE FOR PARENTS

Stafford* voiced that diagnosis and counseling are one continuing process and should begin simultaneously. It is of prime importance that professional staff members involved in the diagnostic process also be included in counseling. He stressed the importance of including parents from the inception to the conclusion of the diagnostic and treatment process. Diagnostic information is of little use to parents unless it can be adjusted to fit into the parents' short- and long-range plans for care of the child. Parents should participate in present and future treatment plans.

Since most parents with retarded children suffer from some emotional conflicts, guidance and counseling are deemed important if the child is to be effectively treated. Parents must either change their method of viewing the child or develop ego defense mechanisms such as denial, repression or a guilt complex.† Parents must be helped to deal with their feelings. Unless professional help is given, there exists a great likelihood that the emotional problems of the child will increase. For best results both parents should be included in the counseling process.

Through various guidance and counseling techniques provided by diagnostic clinics, parents can be given professional information about their child. The information, if properly introduced, will do much to change the parents' attitudes about their retarded child. Support and guidance by the clinic's professional staff are of vital importance in teaching the parents effective methods of dealing

*Stafford, Diagnosing and Counseling of the Mentally Retarded, *op. cit.,* pp. 151-155.
†David B. Rykamn and Robert Henderson, "The Meaning of a Retarded Child to His Parents: A Focus for Counselors," *Mental Retardation, 3*(1), (August, 1965), p. 4.

with the child as well as their own emotional problems. The diversity of parental problems negate that many specialists be involved in the counseling process, depending upon the unique needs of the parents. Equally important will be the acceptance of the school program by parents. This involvement can be proliferated by including the parents in the educational process through assisting in school related projects and guidance for helping their children with school assignments. It is of prime importance that this type of relationship be evident if the retardate is to achieve maximum benefit from his school program.

COUNSELING AND GUIDANCE FOR THE RETARDED

The mentally retarded need guidance and placement services if they are to achieve satisfactory postschool adjustment. Economic life today presents many difficulties to the mentally retarded. They find themselves constantly in contact and often in competition with persons of higher intellectual abilities. Unless some guidance service is given them, when they embark upon a vocational career, there is a likelihood that their mental handicap will prevent them from adjusting and competing successfully with the more intellectually favored individuals. If the handicapped receive a series of disappointments and failures, much of the effort of the school in helping them become useful citizens will be undone. The principal, social worker, and all the teaching staff as a whole should play informal or formal parts in the philosophy of continuous guidance; all will be important to the total concept.

The school can assist the mentally retarded in making a successful start in the world of work. Kirk and Johnson indicated that vocational or occupational guidance is very important for the mentally handicapped. When the program is directed by a highly trained person, he can be of valuable assistance to the teacher. If the school has no guidance program, the teacher must function as the guidance counselor. Some of his duties will include surveying the community for available jobs, making employer contacts, and gathering information about the various jobs in the community.* Conferences with both prospective employers and employees by

---

*Kirk and Johnson, *Educating the Retarded Child, op. cit.,* pp. 218-223.

the teacher or guidance counselor can prepare the way for the first job. The initial step is very important for both the individuals concerned and the community. The mentally retarded, having completed their compulsory school education, need to continue to develop a sense of worthiness and to realize the effectiveness of their school experiences. Failure at this point may make school experiences seem worthless to them, with resultant loss of self-confidence. Diversion to less socially acceptable patterns of behavior to regain self-confidence may follow.

The community is shown the worth of the school's programs for the retarded when handicapped individuals are able to begin their work careers successfully. Understanding and support by the community of the practicality of the school's objectives in educating the mentally retarded can thereby be strengthened. Persons responsible for training programs should consider and plan for the ultimate goal of placement for the mentally retarded. They should be aware of the reported causes of vocational failures and design programs to emphasize desirable behavior patterns. Successful launching of the retarded into the working community can thus give everyone renewed confidence in the ability of the handicapped to succeed when given adequate educational and vocational opportunities.

Studies concerning the employment of retardates have shown that they will probably be working in an unskilled or semiskilled job. It is important that agencies that employ retardates be capable of counseling the retarded in analyzing jobs in terms of their potentialities. Most schools do not have the facilities for adequate follow-up of the retarded after they leave school. Other community and employment agencies must assume the responsibilities of providing guidance, placement and follow-up. However, the schools should be ready to assist when possible for the welfare of the individuals involved as well as for the community's welfare.

Follow-up after placement in a job is often essential. Despite the preparation of the individual for a job, he may face many difficult problems of adjustment by unreasonable and uncooperative attitudes. Guidance workers must help the worker when this occurs by counseling or by some other logical and comprehensive approach to the problems. Placement services should be rendered by the school or some community agency so that the retarded will be able to seek and maintain a job commensurate with his abilities. The retardate should have guidance if he is to receive from the community all that it has to offer him and if he is to be productive member of his community.

A plan for aiding the retarded to adjust successfully to employment may include physical rehabilitation, personal adjustment, counseling, vocational preparation, selective job placement, and thorough follow-up. This plan can be carried out by a vocational rehabilitation center or placement bureau. The individual is guided from the time of his application until he adjusts successfully on the job. Assets and liabilities are carefully evaluated so that there can be an even matching for the individual's capacities and job opportunities.

Effective planning demands that abilities and disabilities of the whole child be considered if he is to reach his optimum growth. The problems of retardation are so intricate and extensive that no one agency should assume the total responsibility for treating, training, or educating them. A concerted effort is needed by many agencies in the community in providing comprehensive care for the retarded. The school's major responsibilities should be: to provide qualified personnel, necessary facilities, and equipment; an instructional program geared to the individual needs of each pupil; assessment and evaluation of community resources that will aid its instructional program; and finally cooperation with other agencies in the community to provide supportive services for meeting the many needs of retarded children.

CHAPTER 8

HOW CAN PARENTS ENHANCE THEIR ROLE IN FOSTERING THE GROWTH AND DEVELOPMENT OF RETARDED CHILDREN?

FOR the retarded child the type of relationship that exists between the parent and the child is of vital importance. The retarded child does not live in a vacuum. He needs, as do all people, a close emotional relationship if he is to achieve his maximum potentialities. Parental reactions to mental retardation are important, not only for the welfare of the child but for the welfare of the parents themselves and the entire family group.

When a parent discovers that his or her child is retarded the initial reaction varies. Some reactions are of guilt, fear, and hate. Parents of retarded children go through many crises from the initial stages of awareness on through the growth period of the child. While working out the crises many parents have adopted philosophies in order to survive. Many have searched for the cause. Why? What? When?

The relationship between a retarded child and his family is not only more complex and ambivalent than the ordinary one, but also more intense and prolonged. There are many types of adjustment that the parent and family must overcome for wholesome relationships to be established.

IMPACT OF RETARDED CHILDREN ON THE FAMILY STRUCTURE

Rothstein* indicated that virtually all parents of retarded children experience some type of emotional upset and anxiety

*Jerome H. Rothstein, *Mental Retardation: Reading and Resources,* (N.Y., Holt, Rinehart and Winston, 1963).

when they learn that they have a retarded children. The problem is compounded with varying degrees of retardation. Many parents withdraw from active civic life. To some parents, unfortunately, the blow is so severe as to permanently disrupt family relations. Such blows to family companionship and solidarity sometimes affect the other normal children in the family. The experience of being the parent of a retarded child sometimes is so disturbing that even religious faith has been taxed.

Kirk* suggested that the presence of a mentally retarded child in a family unit has far-reaching effects. Kirk, Hutt, and Gibby† point out that the child lives in a culture and environment of which he is a part. His intellectual, emotional, and other behavioral reactions are, in some measure, dependent on his environment. Many factors, particularly those of the child's immediate environment, can interfere with the adequate growth and expression of his intellectual potentials.

For the family of a retarded child, the situation is complicated and hazardous. The particular handicaps of the child, the slowness of his development, the necessity of special arrangements for his physical care, training, and companionship, and the adjustments which must be made in the family's expectations for the future, combine to create pressure on the parents which tends to disrupt the normal family equilibrium. Added to this pressure may be tensions created by the child's difficulties in interpersonal relationships, his slowness to learn, his immature self-control, and his handicap in communication. At the same time, the parent-child relationship is intensified by the child's prolonged immaturity and isolation from a peer group. In some instances, the child will remain emotionally and economically dependent upon his family throughout his life.

Thus, the relationship between a retarded child and his family is not only more complex and ambivalent than the ordinary one, but also more intense and prolonged. Parents of a retarded child often need help in dealing with their family situation, in recognizing and accepting the child's handicaps, and in handling certain day-to-day

---

*Samuel Kirk, *Educating the Retarded Child*, (Boston, Houghton-Mifflin, 1951).
†Max L. Hutt and Robert W. Gibby, *The Mentally Retarded Child: Development, Education and Treatment*, (Boston, Allyn & Bacon, 1965).

problems of living with both this child and his normal brothers and sisters. (*See* Appendix G, pp. 139-146.)

PARENTAL REACTIONS

As in the case of any human being, the retarded child doesn't live in a vacuum. According to Baumeister* the retarded child needs, as do all persons, a close emotional relationship with others and these relationships must be satisfying and stress-reducing if he is to achieve his maximum potentialities. Further, as with all children, the relationships between the retarded child and his parents are of great importance. If the parents manifest negative personality reactions to the child's deficient abilities, then it becomes more difficult for wholesome relationships to be established. The greater the negative reactions of the parents, the less likely it is that the child will achieve the level of emotional maturity he is capable of attaining. Negative reactions of the parents, thus, can adversely affect the full maturational process of the retardate.

Rothstein† reflected that when parents recognize the extent to which their child is retarded, they attempt to seek the cause of the seeming tragedy which has beset them. Two types of motivation seem to underlie this search. The first and more rational approach is a hope that in discovering the etiology of the disorder, a way might be found that will cure the retardate and prevent the occurrence of retardation in any future children they may have. Additional motivation for the research probably stems from an ardent wish for relief from a heavy burden of responsibility and guilt. One way or another, a great many parents feel that the blame for their child's handicap rests with them. They may, for example, be concerned because they allowed the baby to roll off the bed or failed to call a physician when he was ill. Still others harbor the memory of an unwanted pregnancy, sometimes even of a deliberate attempt to abort the unwanted fetus. In many parents, the most primitive kinds of thinking determine beliefs

---

*Alfred A. Baumeister, *Mental Retardation,* (Chicago, Aldine Publishing Company, 1967).
†Rothstein, *op. cit.,* 1963.

about the etiology of the handicap. Sometimes the retarded child becomes the focus of all past wrongdoings of which the parents feel ashamed. Parents who thus blame themselves for their child's handicap suffer an additional burden which takes its own trail.

Not only do some parents see a connection between the retarded child and pre- and extra-marital transgressions, but unusual intra-marital sex practices and intercourse late in pregnancy are felt to give rise to this conflict. The conflict is proliferated when the parent sees the retarded child as an extension of himself. Ryckman and Henderson* wrote that there are six areas of meaning involved in the parent-child relationship, particularly as it relates to the ego-extension view. These areas are:

1. The parent considers the child as a physical and psychological extension of himself.
2. The child is a means of vicarious satisfaction to the parents.
3. The parents can derive some measure of immortality through their children.
4. The child is involved in the concept of a personalized love object.
5. There is a parental feeling of worth in responding to the dependency needs of the child.
6. The parents can express negative feelings about the limitations and demands of child rearing.

In summation, the author concluded that the underlying factors of parental expectations of having a child are positive values as an ego-extension and anticipation of the birth of a normal, healthy child. Consequently, most parents perceive a retarded child as a dissapointment and a direct blow to their ego.

SIBLING INTEGRATION

There is no doubt that sibling initial reactions will be influenced by the approach utilized by the parents in relating the problem associated with the mentally retarded. One important consideration in this respect is the age of the sibling in relation to his ability to grasp the meaning of those factors related to mental retardation, and the capacity to understand the ramifications,

---

*David B. Ryckman and Robert A. Henderson, "The Meaning of a Retarded Child to his Parents: A focus for Counselors," *Mental Retardation, 3,* 1965.

limitations, and avenues available to deal with this problem.

Fowle* found in her study that the role tension of the sibling in the family, especially that of the oldest female, tended to be higher when the retarded child was kept in the home than when he had been placed in a residential hospital. What seems to be significant in Fowle's study is that perhaps the oldest female sibling's internalized anxieties were based on a preconceived notion that her role as oldest female member would be burdened by additional responsibilities in caring for her mentally retarded brother or sister. If this were the case, additional frustrations might mount in relation to the lack of knowledge specific to the child's needs in caring for him. Further, one cannot overlook the possibility that the oldest female's role tension might originate from a fear that she may bear a similar child when she assumes her marital role.

Barsch† has pointed out that "the sibling of the brain-damaged child tend to imitate their parents" explanations when talking to their playmates; and the matter of sibling explaining the brain-damaged youngster to their peers and friends is apparently not a significant problem in the eyes of the parent. This statement somewhat supports the authors contention that the parents explanation and subsequent attitudes toward their deficient child will influence sibling attitudes. In addition, the marital relationships between the parents, i.e. harmony-disharmony, will have a formidable impact on sibling attitudes and perceptions vis-a-vis appropriate roles within the family, and the vying for parental affections that already exist. Siblings may assume a feeling of jealousy in that the parents may direct their concerns toward the mentally retarded child, tending to ignore the affectional needs of the other normal children.

If this occurs, the jealousy can turn into hate toward the handicapped child since he has become an obstruction to the normal parent-sibling relationship. On the other hand, siblings may become very pitying toward their mentally retarded sibling if the

---

*C. M. Fowle, "Effects of the Severely Mentally Retarded Child on His Family," *American Journal of Mental Deficiency*, *73*, 1968, pp. 468-73.
†R. H. Barsch, "Explanations Offered by Parents and Siblings of Brain-Damaged Children," *Exceptional Children*, 1961, *27*, pp. 286-91.

parents exhibit an attitude that this child is helpless and thus the only way he will survive in world is through our constant care and concern. If the parents assume an air of total rejection for this child, it would seem that the siblings also will tend in this direction.

What appears to be important here is that the sibling's acceptance and harmonious integration of his mentally retarded brother or sister will primarily be influenced by the parental adaptation to the problem. Although there may be some inner-anxieties resulting from the sibling's rationalization of the problem, the eventual integration of an adjustment to the mentally retarded child will be primarily influenced by parental guidance, understanding, and appropriate child-rearing techniques used. The attitudes and actions of over-protectiveness, authoritarianism, etc., will no doubt influence sibling role functioning. The emphasis then is that the parents, in their efforts to provide the essential ingredients to cope with their mentally retarded child, must not lose sight of their responsibility to the other normal siblings.

THE EXTENDED FAMILY

There may be a few instances where the family feels shame; particularly if it is one that takes pride in its "good stock." The reactions of the grandparents, more than the other members of the family, is very significant and will influence the attitudinal roles of the appropriate parent to whom they are aligned. For example, they may feel that the child's pathology had origins within their own lineage or, they may project the blame onto the lineage of the son- or daughter-in-law. What could then follow is an attempt to rationalize the problem, such as, "From the beginning, I knew this marriage was wrong — I had this funny feeling — now this event has supported my original suspicions."

Much research is needed to explore the reactions of the extended family members and how these impinge upon the parents involved. We can only assume that their attitudes will be similar to the parents in a variety of ways. Even though they themselves did not experience the "birth" of the abnormal child they nonetheless must feel a part of it.

If a parent has strong ties with any particular family member, how that member handles the situation will significantly influence what course of action the parent will take, and perhaps even affect the future relationship between them.

The conclusion that can be drawn is that the reactions of the extended family will influence and contribute to the attitudes of the parents both initially and on a continuing basis. What is necessary here is love, understanding, assistance, and encouragement by the family to the parents and ultimately to the retarded child. With the family's support, the parents will be able to take some comfort in knowing that the family is interested in both them and the child. The parents are looking for strength during this crisis. The family's encouragement and support just may be the catalyst that is needed to assist the parents in adjusting to their problem.

THE EXTENDED COMMUNITY

Social factors have a great deal of influence on the adjustment processes that parents will make concerning their mentally retarded child. These factors usually do not bear upon the initial reactions of the parents but they do affect the later decisions and coping techniques in conjunction with those of the physician, extended family, and religious affiliation.

The parents obviously place great emphasis on what society feels toward their mentally retarded child, particularly the community segment to which it belongs. Frustrations are increased then when the parents attempt to project what they perceive as society's expectations of them, their abnormal child, and the course of action that should be taken. The integration process of the views of society and the extended family, in relations to the parents, places added strain on the parental perceptions of the child and may, if these views tend to be polarized, create conflicts as to the proper course of action.

Parental acceptance or rejection of their retarded child is thus compounded by the attitudes they hold as well as those attitudes and the value systems expressed by the social environment to which they are aligned. Zuk* generalized by saying that society tends naturally to disapprove of those individuals who will not be able to maintain standards. The family of the handicapped child is faced with a societal ambivalence toward its problem. The extent of the painfulness seems again to depend at least to some degree on cultural factors. It is understandable that the parent who is highly conscious of social standards of behavior will tend to have an especially difficult time.

In contrast to Zuk's study, that of Appell† indicated that parents felt the community understood and accepted their retarded children. Similarly, Condell** found that parents were rather satisfied with the attitudes and behavior of their neighbors in relation to the retarded child. Thurston's†† findings indicated that 74 percent of the parents interviewed in his study related that they felt free to discuss their handicapped children with friends and neighbors. However, their responses frequently conveyed the impression that they were very sensitive and were almost daring anyone to say something wrong to them. The aftermentioned research has shown that the social views and attitudes between parents and community will have a bearing upon the ultimate role of the retarded child in the community. One is supportive of the other and will affect future views through cohesive efforts in adapting to the problem.

The retarded child himself suffers in unfortunate ways from the lack of awareness on the part of the general public and the neglect of his welfare. At times he finds himself so overprotected by his baffled parents that he is prevented from developing his abilities. On the other hand, a few extremely harassed parents may subconsciously reject him and he may become fearful and deeply plagued by inferiority feelings. Oftentimes, the schools deny him

*G. H. Zuk, "Cultural Dilemna and Spiritual Crisis of the Family with a Handicapped Child," *Exceptional Children, 28,* 1962, pp. 405-8.

†M. J. Appell, C. M. Williams, and K. N. Fishell, "Changes in Attitudes of Parents of Retarded Children Effected Through Group Counseling," *American Journal of Mental Deficiency, 68,* 1964, pp. 807-12.

**J. F. Condell, "Parental Attitudes Toward Mental Retardation," *American Journal of Mental Deficiency, 71,* 1966, pp. 85-92.

††J. R. Thurston, "Counseling the Parents of the Severely Handicapped," *Exceptional Children, 26,* 1960, pp. 351-54.

the opportunity for training that would enable him to live as a productive citizen.

A healthy community reaction can lessen the dismay and the feeling of utter loneliness and helplessness that parents suffer on learning that, because of a birth accident or another cause, their child is retarded.

COUNSELING PARENTS

Research findings have consistently shown that virtually all parents experience some source of anxiety when a retarded child is present in the family. According to Robinson and Robinson* there are special problems faced by parents of retarded children. Parents go through many stages of adjustment to the fact that their child is retarded. Awareness of the fact confirming retardation may likely cause intense subconscious anger on the part of the parents and development of an innate pattern of parental rejection of the child. Parents often have difficulty coping with these feelings. Even the most mature parents find these subconscious reactions troublesome. While parents differ in their initial reaction, most display helplessness, grief, or guilt in varying degrees. The passage of time has apparently done little to ameliorate this condition.

The initial impact of a retarded child can be severe and profound; parental coping can be unsuccessful or incomplete; and repeated crises may arise. Many parents may thus suffer from poor mental health. Some of the mechanisms by which this might come about have already been indicated. For most parents of retardates there is the lack of acceptance of their child. Often the retarded child is perceived as an intruder, and his relationship with his parents is frequently fraught with frustration, doubts, fears, guilt, and anger. These barriers combine to prevent the healthy integration of the retarded child into the family structure.

In order for most retarded children to be successfully integrated into the family structure, parents will need some form of counseling. Counseling will enable the parent to view the child in a

*H. B. Robinson and N. H. Robinson, *The Mentally Retarded Child: A Psychological Approach,* (New York, McGraw-Hill Co., 1965), pp. 506-23.

different perspective. Unless professional help is given there exists a great likelihood that the emotional problems of both child and parents will increase. Professional personnel can serve a valuable function in showing parents how to deal effectively with their retarded children. It should be noted that all professionals are not trained to counsel parents of retarded children; however, they can serve as agents in the referring process.

Theoretically, the professional therapist or counselor is the ideal person to counsel parents. The psychological problems, although different in focus, should be amenable to traditional therapeutic techniques. However, there are some who are hindered by their traditional approach to therapeutic problems. Many times parents require assistance immediately and a flexible approach involving prolonged contact may not be necessary.* Research findings by Reid and Shyne† have indicated that short-term therapy for crisis intervention can produce effective results. The psychological state of the parents, age, number of children, and sex of the retarded child are some of the factors that will determine the type and degree of counseling. Therefore, the counselor/therapist should be highly trained and competent in his field in order that he might appropriately guide the parent.

The role of the school in providing counseling services for retarded children and their parents has been outlined in previous chapters. When the psychological problems of parents with retarded children are too complex for the school to handle, the mental health specialists might have to assist the school. In this respect the role of the school is one of cooperation and coordination.

COMMUNITY AND PARENTAL INVOLVEMENT

It is commonly stated that no school program can be completely effective without the support of parents and the community. When parents and community become actively

---

*Kathryn P. Meadow and Lloyd Meadow, "Changing Role Perceptions for Parents of Handicapped Children" *Exceptional Children, 38,* 1971, pp. 24-25.
†W. J. Reid and A. W. Shyne, "Brief and Extended Casework," (New York, Columbia University Press, 1969).

involved in the school program, the entire educational program for retarded children and their parents benefit. It becomes quite clear that when the school and community are genuinely interested in the welfare of the retarded child and his parents, apathy and despair succumb to hope and self-fulfillment, which can do much to ease many of the emotional problems experienced. Further, improvement in communication can do much to eliminate the negativism that many parents have developed. This positive approach cannot but assist the retarded child in his educational pursuits.

A desirable relationship in the community is one which is marked by a strong bond of understanding and cooperation between parents and school personnel. Parents should have a direct share in deciding what types of instruction appear to serve their children best. Parents should be welcome to make suggestions for the guidance of their children. Through various channels the school should enlist the cooperation of parents and community agencies in designing and implementing educational programs for retarded children. As Baumgartner* has stated, "In communities where educators work with parents and with religious, recreational, and social agencies in a constructive effort to help, the results are reflected in healthier personalities of boys and girls."

---

*Baumgartner, *op. cit.,* p. 149.

CHAPTER 9

WHAT IS THE PROMISE
OF THE FUTURE?

PROBLEMS of education for retarded children have undergone radical changes in the last decades. Today the school assumes the responsibility of educating retarded children. Special methods and provisions are being made to enable retarded children to reach their optimum level of growth. Many of the preceding chapters have dealt directly or indirectly with providing equal educational opportunities for retarded children. This chapter will deal primarily with new directions and plans for the future.

With the vast amount of money being appropriated by local, state, and federal government, increased research in all fields related to retarded children, improved teacher training, increased services to retarded children and their families, and legislation for the support of programs for retarded children, may lead us to conclude that educational opportunities are finally being achieved. However, in spite of intervention from several sources and tremendous gains accomplished in the last two decades, there is a preponderance of retarded children whose needs are not being adequately met in the public schools. There are those who are denied effective education and services to ameliorate their handicapping conditions. One of the major conceptual problems to be faced in providing quality education for retarded persons is to gear programs toward their unique needs.

In the position paper adopted by The Council for Exceptional Children,* it was pointed out that the educational opportunities provided by the schools have tended to neglect or exclude children with unusual learning needs. These children need special education and specialized diagnostic and instructional services in order to be

*See page 17.

able to benefit fully from education. Because of their unique needs, retarded children need to begin their school experiences earlier, many need educational services well into adulthood, and many require health and social services that are closely coordinated with school programs.

Providing equal educational opportunities for retarded children is intricate and extensive. A concerted effort should be made by the schools to coordinate many of the activities in the community. The schools are in a unique position to achieve this major goal as well as to solve many of the issues concerning education and services for retarded children. Consequently, the schools should assume a leadership role in the community. It would appear that a strong department of special education, with competent personnel, facilities, and finance, would do much to minimize pressure from community groups demanding that equal educational opportunities be provided for retardates. Further, a strong department of special education would be in a unique position to take the leadership in coordinating services in the community.

IMPROVING THE EDUCATION OUTLOOK
FOR RETARDED CHILDREN

The aim of special education for the retarded is basically the same aim as that of all education: to teach the individual how to live better; to teach him to use all of his capacities; and to teach him to become a useful member of his social group. The nature of the retarded child's handicaps limits both the amount and kind of subject matter. Much of the personal and social progress made must be on a habit formation basis. The objectives of a public school program for retarded children should be to develop social competencies, occupational adequacy, and academic learning to the limit of the child's ability.

The basic characteristic of mentally retarded children is mental limitations. They are limited in adapted power, in associate power, and in learning speed. The retarded child must spend much time learning and practicing the simple things that the normal child picks up casually. The school must realize that each retarded individual has a potential, and must take the child as it finds him and help him grow through his school experiences. Additionally, the school program should continue as long as the individual benefits from its experiences.

Until recently it was generally conceived that profoundly retarded children could not benefit substantially from teaching efforts, regardless of the method employed. Recent research has proven this widely accepted concept to be in error. Empirical studies have shown that the profoundly retarded can be taught self-help skills by using a combination of innovative techniques and procedures broken down into small steps and reinforced systematically. As a result of empirical research, coupled with demands from community and parent groups, educational provisions for profoundly retarded children have accelerated tremendously in the last few decades.

In order that the present trends may be strengthened and promulgated, the school must concern itself with some of the immediate problems, such as improved pupil identification and placement, facilities, teacher and related school personnel preparation, guidance, curriculum design, and special services, if the retarded child is going to realize the full impact of his education.

SELECTION AND PLACEMENT

The selection and placement of pupils in appropriate classes is an important facet of the total special education program. Proper placement can result only when there is a thorough group screening, a comprehensive individual evaluation, an understanding of characteristics of the retarded, and workable criteria for placement. Much confusion and misunderstanding can be prevented by having well defined lines of authority for making the final decision about placement of children. Meeting the needs of mentally retarded children covers a broad spectrum of services. It is generally agreed that children with special classroom needs should be served by the regular classroom, if the regular classroom can meet their needs. However, it might be necessary to place some retarded children in community based programs or special classes, depending upon the needs as well as what type of placement will assure educational opportunities for them. Administrators should be cognizant of the fact that wherever retarded children are placed, they will need supportive or supplementary services if they are going to reach their full optimum growth.

All placement should be flexible, allowing the retarded children to move from various educational settings as his needs dictate. School systems that place retarded children in various educational settings based solely on the results or IQ test results, are denying retarded children their basic democratic rights to equal education. Proper placement can only result if objective evaluations are completed. All placement should indicate a possible time table when the retarded child can be integrated into the regular class if he has a potential for success in the regular classroom. (*See* Appendix F, p. 138)

Consultation with parents or guardians is necessary whenever placement of an exceptional child is made into or out of a special program.

FACILITIES, EQUIPMENT AND SUPPLIES

The type and variety of equipment and supplies involved in teaching retarded children are dictated to a large degree by the budget, the age of the children, and the ability of school personnel to plan appropriately. Teachers and administrators should not overlook two valuable sources for securing additional equipment and materials which the budget may not permit. The first is from community organizations. In many cases organizations have given teachers of retarded children substantial sums of money to spend for classroom materials. A second valuable source is the actual construction of materials by children, by parents, members of the community, and the teacher. Teaching materials such as educational games, doll clothes, toys, book shelves, and furniture are examples of things which can be made, often by vocational high school students. Simpler articles can be made by the retarded children themselves. With imagination and ingenuity a teacher can help direct and guide a successful self-help program. (*See* Appendix C, pp. 132-133)

Classrooms for the mentally retarded should permit them to plan, experiment, read, create, play, and share their experiences in reasonable comfort and safety. A good classroom for retarded children should also have an adequate amount and variety of equipment and supplies that can be used for carrying on significant real life activities. If facilities are not provided in the retardates' classroom, it might be necessary for them to go to specially equipped rooms elsewhere.

The location of classrooms is as important as its size and furnishings. An acceptable classroom is in an area that is not isolated or remote from the rest of the school and that is without suggestion of stigmatization or discredit. The location of the class, as well as lighting, ventilation and general appearance, is expected to be at least as satisfactory as that of any classroom in the school.

A classroom to be used for general nonmanual and quieter manual activities needs suitable equipment. Individual, movable, silenced desks and chairs to permit flexibility of classroom planning and arrangement are desirable. A large amount of materials and objects that are needed for manual and academic experiences should be easily accessible and provide children with ample shelf and cabinet space. A sufficient number of bulletin, chalk, and exhibit boards are required for needed demonstration and exhibition purposes. It is important that provisions be made for a classroom book corner which pupils may use as a resource for information and pleasure. The well-equipped classroom should also include audio-visual equipment that can widen and enrich children's experiences. Additional requirements for a classroom include these provisions: ready access to lavoratories and showers, a suitable nearby outdoor play area, and easy access to a garden if one can be provided. (*See* Appendix B, pp. 129-131)

COMPETENT SCHOOL PERSONNEL

Selection of qualified school personnel to teach and administer school programs for retarded children is of utmost importance. Personnel must be well informed and specially trained to work with retarded children.

Preparation for a director of special education in general would call for educational training of a nature similar to that of an assistant director or supervisor but more comprehensive. High standards are needed for the selection of directors and supervisors of a special education program for the mentally retarded. Furthermore, an examining board that is impartial, well-qualified and capable is an essential prerequisite. With the selection of the most capable administrators possible, teachers of the mentally retarded can be given maximum help in achieving the goals of education with these children.

As mentioned earlier, a large share of the responsibility for direct supervision of the special class for mentally retarded children lies with the principal. His efforts, coordinated with those of the department of special education, are directed toward studying and improving the total teaching-learning situation of which the mentally retarded are a part. He takes into account both instructional and administrative problems, recognizing that the life-centered curriculum of the special class is affected by all factors in the school situation. The principal should act cooperatively with special class teachers to obtain better understanding of the basic principles and policies underlying the education of mentally retarded children. He should act to release and coordinate the creative abilities of these teachers and encourage them to seek constantly better ways of meeting the needs of children with a mental handicap.

The principal, in cooperation with the special class supervisor, uses both group and individual techniques in helping teachers of the mentally retarded improve the total teaching-learning situations. The special class teachers are provided opportunities for working together both as a special-interest group and as members of other groups that include regular class teachers, depending upon purposes. Group techniques may include the cooperative study of instructional and administrative problems, study groups, local workshops, and group study of the community. Individual techniques include the principal's visits to the special classroom followed by conferences, visits of teachers to other special classes both in and outside of their school, promotion of activities that capitalize on the special interests of the teachers, and stimulation of continued professional development through attendance of special class teachers at colleges and universities. Special class teachers thus can have opportunities, through group and individual activities, to study and improve the teaching and learning of mentally retarded children. They also have an opportunity to contribute to better understanding by regular classroom teachers of the problems faced in special classes for the mentally retarded and their relation to the total school program.

The key position of the principal in improving the educational program for the mentally retarded requires that he have a basic understanding of the characteristics and needs of these exceptional children and of the modifications and adaptations required in the total school program for these children. The professional preparation of the principal should not be lacking in the area of special preparation for exceptional children.

Teachers of retarded children should be carefully selected. High standards of personal fitness and professional preparation should determine selection, not mere administrative expediency. Some school districts require prospective special teachers to take both an oral and written examination, together with health tests and performance tests. Many school systems require a probationary period of one or more years, before permanent appointment is made. Special supervisory assistance is given during the probationary year(s).

Whatever the procedure for selection, teachers who are appointed should be able to give mentally retarded children the best educational opportunities possible for happy, successful living. In the absence of a year of special training in the education of the mentally retarded, as part of the undergraduate teacher preparation course, newly appointed special class teachers are expected to have had at least a year of successful teaching experiences as a regular teacher. This experience is considered essential in order that the teacher be able to evaluate properly the achievement of children with low IQ's. Regular class experience is helpful, also, in giving the teacher an opportunity to decide if he has the interest and ability to work with pupils having exceptional problems.

Since special education, regardless of opinions which justify or refute its existence, it is an established division of public school education; and because of the critical learning factors involved, a considerable amount of money appropriated by federal and state governments is earmarked for use with special education endeavors on a pupil ratio basis. It seems apparent that special education personnel must possess competencies that will enable them to be fluent and efficient in educational spheres. Certification and qualification should not be any different than those required of education in other fields; in many instances standards should be higher. Personnel who are lacking in ability and specific training for meeting the needs of retarded children will in all probability deprive them of the right kinds of school experiences necessary for the best possible life adjustments. Teachers and administrators require instructional skills not usually required for the regular grades. Great emphasis should be placed on the use of a variety of media in instructing retarded children.

GUIDANCE

Guidance for retarded children is no different from that of normal children, that is to help the child achieve personal and social growth through a better understanding of himself. Methods and techniques for achieving this end with retarded children may need to be altered because of these children's unique needs. Guidance is a continuous process that should start when the child first enters school and expands throughout his school career. All school personnel should participate in the philosophy of a continuous guidance program for the retardates. If no guidance personnel are available in the school, the teacher should assume direct responsibility for providing sound guidance principles for his class.

CURRICULUM DESIGN

Curriculum means all the planned experiences provided by the school to assist pupils in attaining the designated learning outcome to the best of their abilities. It bridges the past, present, and the future. The curriculum should be designed to:

1. develop the child's mental capabilities.
2. strengthen the child's emotional stability.
3. fulfill the child's health and social needs.
4. promote the child's occupational adjustment.

The implementation of the above objectives into practical curriculum activities is mandatory in preparing an adequate way of life for the retarded in our society. Curriculum in its development depends upon numerous factors. Considerations must be given to the intellectual learning potential of the retarded as well as to aims and objectives of education.

The schools must provide systematic and appropriate methods of assessing the impact of its instruction on retarded children, through the formation of realistic objectives based upon needs, capacities and interests of the mentally retarded. Many retarded children can be helped to talk, read and figure with the competency needed for adequate everyday living. They will require considerably more drill and practice in skills and habits than is required for most children if their living is to be effective. Plentiful quantities of opportunities for making concrete applications of their ideas is important since they do not express themselves well verbally or in abstract ways. It is also important that activities help retarded children gain honest and realistic appraisals of themselves so that their life's goals will be set neither too high nor too low.

The curriculum must be derived from the intensive study of the individual child. It must provide for the setting and climate in which the child can grow and develop his capacities, regardless of his mental abilities. To accomplish this end, school personnel must have an open and objective mind. They must be alter to even the most subtle cues as the children react to their experiences. Additionally, administrators should be flexible enough to reject their favorite theories or techniques when their application fails.

During the past decade, special educators have been concerned with curriculum development for the retarded. Meyen* gives brief statements from several writers on curriculum development for the mentally retarded.

> Thorsell (1969) concluded after an evaluation of numerous curriculum guides that they resulted in teaching practices that were indicative of haphazard selection of unit topics, many of which regular class sources, where as others were greatly outdated unit topics that had been abstracted from other guides written for the use with the mentally retarded; "Many curriculum guides for the mentally

---

*Edward L. Meyen, "Curriculum Development for Exceptional Children: A Focus on Evaluation," *Focus on Exceptional Children, 1,* 1969, pp. 1-4.

retarded are watered down traditional school guides is supported by
the study of Simches and Bohn" (1963). They examined over 250
curriculum guides for the mentally retarded from which they reported
a serious lack of scope and sequence of content unit. They concluded
that the special class curriculum is in reality not distinctive, but only
watered down versions of the regular school curriculum. The writers
found the same criticisms in reviewing over 125 curriculum guides for
the mentally retarded. In addition, it was observed that many of the
guides were cut-and-paste jobs which tended to modify the Illinois
Curriculum Guide developed by Goldstein and Seigle (1958).

If the school is to assist retardates in achieving social and
vocational competencies, it is essential that a special developmental curriculum be provided for them. Activities should be
sequenced into small steps where the retarded will have a chance
to succeed. Since retardates learn best from concrete materials, as
many concrete experiences as possible should be provided. Criteria
for the selection of curricular content should be based on an
understanding of the retarded, provided through research findings
and observation. Equally important will be assessing the present
and future job market in order to assure the retardate a place in
the world to work after his school experiences.

SPECIAL SERVICES

A wide range of services should be evident for retarded children,
including assistance from various disciplines, to aid school
personnel in providing quality education. Many problems are too
complex for the school to handle alone. The services of specialists
can bring to the classroom enrichment for the children that the
school could not otherwise provide. Services for mentally retarded
children should be improved in the area of diagnosis, evaluation,
and treatment. Special services should be an integral part of the
teaching-learning program for retarded children. A comprehensive
system of services for retarded children should be coordinated
with other agencies in the community. The principal should be the
key person charged with this responsibility. Other types of services
that schools should provide are in the areas of transportation,
specially designed facilities, special equipment, individualized
instruction, and supportive teaching personnel. These are to name

but a few services needed to meet the individual differences of retardates.

In summary, the schools must produce retarded citizens who have been trained and educated for special competencies and have been given some direction and preparation for occupational competency. In reviewing records of adult retardates, it becomes evident that the schools have not provided many retarded individuals with the skills to compete successfully in our society. When one attempts to assess the reasons for the school's failure, it becomes a complex process. However, in this connection, many goals and training programs implemented by the schools are badly disguised, unscientifically selected, and culturally unsuitable for retarded children. Another factor might be a lack of clear analysis of the tasks involved. Thus, the chief aim of the school should be to shape attitudes toward goals which are acceptable to retardates and reflect his present and future needs. It is not likely that this objective can be achieved by the school alone, parents and community agencies must be fully involved.

When followed, the basic guides that have been enumerated and discussed can help achieve these major results: (1) the organization of adequately staffed and equipped classes as a result of careful, cooperative planning with the guidance and cooperation of a department of special education; (2) the use of sound pupil personnel procedures that are based on knowledge and understanding of the needs and characteristics of the mentally retarded; (3) the provision of needed supervisory services to aid teachers and principals of classes for the mentally retarded in improving instruction; (4) the development of a well-integrated program of special services to meet the individual differences of mentally retarded pupils; and (6) the fostering of school-community relationships that will aid in the understanding and support of a special education program for these handicapped pupils. Underlying the achievement of desired results should be adequate financial support, cooperative action, and continuous evaluation by the school and community.

The use of the basic guides is urged since the quality of conditions and services provided for the mentally retarded by the school affects in large measure the quality of their living and learning. Thus mentally retarded pupils will be helped to grow and develop through democratic means. These pupils, from the day of their school entrance to the end of their school careers, will then receive the fullest attention and the best help that the school can give. The highest quality of conditions and services will be made available to them, as to all children, for their maximum growth and development. Then will the investment of public education for the mentally retarded pay rich dividends in their productive and responsible living as respected members of the community.

REFERENCES

General

Anderson, Robert M., Hemenway, Robert E., and Anderson, Janet W.: Instructional Resources for Teachers of the Culturally Disadvantaged and Exceptional. Springfield, Charles C Thomas Publishing Co., 1969.

Baker, Harry J.: Introduction to Exceptional Children, 3rd Ed. New York, The Macmillan Company, 1959.

Barbe, Walter B.: The Exceptional Child. Washington, D.C., Center for Applied Research in Education, 1963.

Connor, Leo E.: Administration of Special Education Programs. New York, Bureau of Publications, Teachers College, Columbia University, 1961.

Cruickshank, W. M., Ed.: Psychology of Exceptional Children and Youth, 3rd Ed. Englewood Cliffs, New Jersey, Prentice-Hall, Inc., 1967.

Cruickshank, W. M. and Johnson, G. O., Ed.: Education of Exceptional Children and Youth, 2nd Ed. Englewood Cliffs, New Jersey, Prentice-Hall, Inc., 1967.

Dunn, Lloyd M., Ed.: Exceptional Children in the Schools. New York, Holt, Rinehart and Winston, Inc., 1963.

Frampton, Merle E., et al.: Forgotten Children: A Program for the Multihandicapped. Boston, Porter Sargent, 1969.

Garrison, K. C., and Force, D. G.: The Psychology of Exceptional Children, 4th Ed. New York, Ronald Press, 1965.

Gearheart, B. R.: Administration of Special Education. Springfield, Charles C Thomas, Publishers, 1967.

Goldberg, I. Ignacy: Selected Bibliography of Special Education. New York, Teachers College, Columbia University, 1967.

Gowan, John Curtis and Demos, George D.: The Guidance of Exceptional Children. New York, David McKay Company, Inc., 1965.

Haring, Norris G. and Schiefelbusch, Richard L., Ed.: Methods in Special Education. New York, McGraw-Hill Book Company, 1967.

Hollmuth, Jerome, Ed.: The Special Child in Century 21. Seattle, Special Child Publications, Inc., 1964.

Johnson, G. Orville and Blank, Harriet D., Ed.: Exceptional Children Research Review. Washington, D.C. The Council for Exceptional Children, 1968.

Jones, Morris Val, Ed.: Special Education Programs Within the United States. Springfield, Charles C Thomas, Publishers, 1968.

Jones, Reginald L., Ed.: New Directions in Special Education. Boston, Allyn and Bacon, Inc., 1970.

Kephart, Newell C.: The Slow Learner in the Classroom. Columbus, Charles E. Merrill Books, Inc., 1960.

Kirk, Samuel A.: Educating Exceptional Children. Boston, Houghton Mifflin Co., 1972.

Lincoln Filene Center: Negro Self-Concept. New York, McGraw-Hill Book Co., 1965.

Mackie, Romaine P.: Special Education in the United States: Statistics 1948-1966. New York, Teachers College Press, Teachers College, Columbia University, 1969.

Orem, Reginald Calvert: Montessori and the Special Child. New York, Capricorn Books, 1970.

Peter, Lawrence J.: Prescriptive Teaching. New York, McGraw-Hill Pub. Co., 1965.

Reger, Roger, et al.: Special Education. New York, Oxford University Press, 1968.

Siegel, Ernest: Special Education in the Regular Classroom. New York, John Day Company, 1969.

Stark, Edward S.: Special Education: A Curriculum Guide. Springfield, Charles C Thomas, Publishers, 1969.

Tannenbaum, Abraham J., Ed.: Special Education and Programs for Disadvantaged Children and Youth. Washington, D.C., The Council for Exceptional Children, 1968.

Trapp, E. P., and Himelstein, P., Ed.: Readings on the Exceptional Children: Research and Theory. New York, Appleton-Century-Crofts, 1962.

Wright, Nathan Jr., Ed.: What Black Educators are Saying. New York, Hawthorn Books Inc., Publishers, 1970.

Mentally Retarded: Educable

Carlson, Bernie Wells and Gingeland, David R.: Play Activities for the Retarded Child. New York, Abingdon Press, 1961.

Charney, Leon and LaCrosse, Edward: The Teacher of the Mentally Retarded. New York, The John Day Company, 1965.

Erdman, Robert L.: Educable Retarded Children in Elementary Schools. Washington, D.C. The Council for Exceptional Children, 1961.

Erickson, Marion J.: The Mentally Retarded Child in the Classroom. New York, The MacMillan Company, 1965.

Garton, Malinda Dean: Teaching the Educable Mentally Retarded, 2nd Ed. Springfield, Charles C Thomas, Publishers, 1964.

Hegeman, Mary Theodore: The Challenge of the Retarded Child, Revised Ed. Milwaukee, Bruce Publishing Company, 1969.

Hutt, Max L. and Gibby, Robert Gwyn: The Mentally Retarded Child, 2nd Ed. Boston, Allyn and Bacon, Inc., 1965.

Ingram, Christine P.: Education of the Slow-Learning Child. 3rd Ed. New York, The Ronald Press Co., 1960.

Johnson, G. Orville: Education for the Slow Learners. Englewood Cliffs, New Jersey, Prentice-Hall, Inc., 1963.

Kirk, Samuel A. and Weiner, Bluma B., Ed.: Behavioral Research on Exceptional Children. Washington, D.C., The Council for Exceptional Children, 1963.

Rothstein, Jerome H., Ed. Mental Retardation. New York, Holt, Rinehart and Winston, 1961.

Slaughter, Stella Stillson: The Educable Mentally Retarded Child and His Teacher. Philadelphia, F. A. Davis Co., 1964.

Sniff, William F.: A Curriculum for the Mentally Retarded Young Adult. Springfield, Charles C Thomas, Publishers, 1962.

Standing, E. M.: Maria Montessori: Her Life and Work. New York, New American Library, 1962.

The President's Panel on Mental Retardation: A Proposed Program for National Action to Combat Mental Retardation. Washington, D.C., U. S. Government Printing Office, October 1962. (Also, read the reports: The Six-Hour Retarded Child, and A Very Special Child, available without charge from The President's Committee on Mental Retardation, Washington, D.C. 20201.)

U. S. Department of Health, Education, and Welfare. Mental Retardation Activities of the Department of Health, Education, and Welfare. Washington, D.C., U. S. Government Printing Office, 1971.

Mentally Retarded: Trainable

Baumeister, Alfred A.: Mental Retardation: Selected Problems in Appraisal, Education and Treatment. Chicago, Aldine-Atherton, Publishers, 1971.

Baumgartner, Bernie B.: Helping the Trainable Mentally Retarded Child. New York, Bureau of Publications, T. C., Columbia University, 1960.

Buck, Pearl S. and Zarfoss, Gwoneth T.: The Gifts They Bring. New York, The John Day Co., 1965.

Connor, Frances P. and Talbot, Mabel E.: An Experimental Curriculum for Young Mentally Retarded Children. New York, Bureau of Publications, Teachers College, Columbia University, 1964.

Frankel, Max G., Happ, William F., and Smith, Maurice P.: Functional Teaching of the Mentally Retarded. Springfield, Charles C Thomas, Publishers, 1966.

Gardner, William I.: Behavior Modification in Mental Retardation. Chicago, Aldine-Atherton, Publishers, 1971.

Itard, J. M. G.: The Wild Boy of Aveyron, Reprint. New York, Appleton-Century-Crofts, Meredith Publishing Co., 1962.

Perry, Natalie: Teaching the Mentally Retarded Child. New York, Columbia University Press, 1960.

Sarason, Seymour B.: Psychological Problems in Mental Deficiency. New York, Harper and Brothers, Publishers, 1949.

Sherman, Mandel: Intelligence and Its Deviations. New York, The Ronald Press, 1945.

Theodore, Sister Mary: The Challenge of the Retarded Child. 2nd Ed. Milwaukee, The Bruce Publishing Co., 1963.

Tredgold, A. F.: A Textbook of Mental Deficiency. 11th Ed. Baltimore, The Williams and Wilkins Company, 1971.

Williams, Harold M.: Education of the Severely Retarded Child: Classroom Programs. Bulletin No. 20. Washington, D.C., U. S. Government Printing Office, 1961.

BASIC SKILLS FOR RETARDED CHILDREN*

1. To teach him to take care of himself, including his personal needs, as well as he can.
2. To help him to perform in as coordinated a manner as he can.
3. To help him to get about in, and become oriented within, as large an area as it is prudently safe for him to traverse.
4. To teach him such skills as he is capable of learning that will be practical or recreationally useful to him.
5. To teach him how to use his leisure time.
6. To teach him to communicate with others as well as he can.
7. To teach him how to work and play with others.
8. To teach him how to become as socially proficient as his mental limitations permit.

SOCIAL INTERACTION SKILLS

I. Self-help skills
   A. Dressing
      1. Can undress self
      2. Can dress self
      3. Puts clothing away neatly
      4. Can manipulate zippers
      5. Can manipulate buttons
      6. Can manipulate snaps
      7. Can manipulate laces
      8. Can manipulate ties
      9. Can manipulate pins
   B. Toilet skills
      1. Asks to use toilet
      2. Washes hands after toileting
      3. Can locate toilet facilities on own
      4. Handles toileting independently
   C. Personal appearance
      1. Washes hands and face
      2. Keeps nose clean
      3. Maintains good posture
      4. Cares for body parts

---

*Compiled by Carole Leavitt, Teacher, D. C. Public Schools. See also Stella/Stillson Slaughter, *The Educable Mentally Retarded Child and His Teacher,* (Philadelphia, F. A. Davis Company, 1964).

    5. Keeps clothes neat and clean
- D. Self-understanding
  1. Knows and can tell his own name
  2. Knows and can tell how old he is
  3. Knows if his family has a telephone
  4. Knows the difference between his and others' belongings
  5. Knows and can tell his house number and the name of the street where he lives
  6. Knows and can tell his apartment number, if he has one
  7. Knows and can tell his phone number
  8. Has personal preferences in games, food, friends, etc.
- E. Manner of play (in sequential order)
  1. Isolated play
  2. Parallel play (near another child)
  3. Associative play (with another child)
  4. In group activity
- F. General social development
  1. Cooperates with teacher
  2. Uses "thank you," "please," etc. appropriately
  3. Shares toys and material
  4. Takes turns
  5. Helps others
  6. Respects rights of others
  7. Accepts disappointments
  8. Accepts suggestions
  9. Accepts criticisms
  10. Accepts failure
  11. Uses appropriate table manners

II. At home
- A. Composition of family
  1. Knows how many people and the relations of the people in his family
  2. Knows the work of various members of his family in the home
  3. Knows the responsibility of an individual to the family
- B. Location of home
  1. Knows the general location of his home
  2. Knows his street address by number and name
  3. Knows the name of the city where he lives
  4. Knows his telephone number
  5. Can get to his home from familiar locations (ex. school, church)
- C. Responsibilities
  1. Knows and carries out chores in the home
  2. Knows rules of cooperation in the family
  3. Knows the roles of the family members which keep the family functioning

D. Function of home
1. Knows the style of home where he lives (ex. apartment, row house)
2. Knows how many rooms in his house
3. Knows the names and uses of particular rooms

III. At school
A. Knows and can tell the names of his classmates
B. Knows how and why we wait our turn
C. Respects property by caring for own
D. Does not make classroom unnecessarily untidy (ex. he does put his own trash in can)
E. Assumes his share of the care of the room
F. Can locate important parts of the school
G. Knows and observes rules of the school
H. Plays successfully with others
I. Is punctual
J. Knows who important people in the school are
K. Knows and observes good conduct on the way to school

IV. In the community
A. Neighborhood
1. Has had experience with places of interest to him (ex. store, police station)
2. Knows the location of and can find his home in the neighborhood
3. Knows what to do if he is lost
4. Knows and can find transportation to get to particular places
5. Knows the meaning of particular signs (ex. exit, walk)
6. Knows the meaning of traffic signals
7. Knows how to ask directions
8. Knows how to read a simple map
9. Knows the following community helpers and how they help us: policeman, milkman, doctor, busdriver, mailman

B. The law
1. Knows the rules of school and home and follows them
2. Has developed habits of honesty, respect for property rights, and readiness to conform to rules in the general interest
3. Knows the traffic rules for drivers and pedestrians
4. Knows the trespass laws
5. Knows the bicycle laws
6. Knows the local regulations which might affect him

C. Public Services
1. Knows how to get to the following services in an emergency: telephone, firemen, police, doctors
2. Knows how to use the following communication services: letters, postal services, telegrams, telephone
3. Knows generally that banks are used for transacting money business

SENSORY TRAINING

Often mentally retarded children have difficulty using their senses to their fullest capacity. The teacher should watch for difficulties in the sensory areas. The amount of training the mentally retarded need in this area is very much an individual matter. A particular child may or may not need the practice of meeting these objectives. At the same time, a child who is weak in one of the senses may need further training.

   I. Vision
      A. After looking at a box with different articles, when the box is removed, the student can name 80 per cent of the objects
      B. Can group objects according to color, size, form, etc.
      C. Can complete puzzles
      D. Can identify and form rhyming words
      E. Can identify and form words with similar beginnings or endings
      F. Can identify and name the colors
  II. Touch
      A. After learning the names of materials, the student can distinguish among materials by touch only
      B. By touch alone, the student can find an object similar to one he has
      C. The student can arrange in sequential order from touch alone
 III. Hearing
      A. Can distinguish and name familiar sounds (ex. telephone, car)
      B. Can clap to various rhythms
      C. While blindfolded, the student can name which classmate is speaking
      D. Gossip game can be played
 IV. Olfactory
      A. Can distinguish among and name some common smells (ex. perfume, vinegar, popcorn, chocolate)
  V. Taste
      A. Can distinguish among and name some familiar tastes
      B. Can tell whether something is hot or cold, bitter or sweet

HEALTH SKILLS

1. Has proper toilet habits
2. Changes underwear daily
3. Brushes teeth properly
4. Willingly and independently takes a bath
5. Knows when one sees the doctor and the dentist
6. Cares for hair by brushing, washing, and fixing
7. Washes hands before and after meals, after toilet, when in contact with food, and at bedtime

8. Knows that different clothes are worn for different occasions and weather
9. Knows what to do in menstruation

SAFETY SKILLS

1. Knows not to touch dangerous objects
2. Stays out of medicine cabinet
3. Knows proper way and rules for riding bicycle
4. Does not leave unless adult knows and has given permission
5. Does not accept rides and gifts from strangers
6. Knows how to call for emergency services on telephone
7. Knows how to get to fire box
8. Knows not to pet stray animals
9. Knows how to use electric appliances
10. Knows how to observe traffic signals and signs
11. Understands the dangers from gas
12. Knows how to put out a small fire
13. Does not leave objects in dangerous spots (ex. toys on stairs)
14. Knows how to board, leave, and act on school bus
15. Obeys school safety patrol
16. Knows who to contact in an emergency

ART

Art should be integrated into the entire school program rather than being left as a subject to itself. In this the activities will be very much dependent on what the class is presently studying, what are the class' interests, and what are the particular abilities of the students at the time.

1. Coloring and drawing
2. Clay modeling
3. Cutting
4. Pasting
5. Finger painting
6. Water or tempera painting
7. Construction
8. Handicrafts
9. Weaving

MUSIC

1. Sing songs with records
2. Listen to records

3. Do exercises to rhythm
4. Play music games
5. Sing songs by rote
6. Make simple instruments
7. Play rhythm instruments
8. Make drawings to illustrate songs and musical stories
9. Dance
10. Listen to music for relaxation
11. Teach names and sounds of various instruments

PHYSICAL EDUCATION

I. Sensory-Motor Skills
   A. Can identify his body parts
   B. Can form spatial relationships (ex. right-left, front-back)
   C. Has developed balance (ex. stand on one foot, walk on balance beam)
   D. Has developed large motor muscles (ex. skipping, tossing objects, sommersaults)
   E. Has developed fine motor muscle coordination (ex. tie shoe, cut with scissors)
II. Recreation Skills
   A. Dancing
   B Swimming
   C. Roller skating
   D. Bicycle riding
   E. Sports

MANUAL ARTS

I. Learn to make things for which the class has a particular need, as defined by individual classes (ex. room decorations, workbooks, desk blinders, flower bed, etc.)
II. Construction and repairing skills
   A. Sawing
   B. Planing
   C. Nailing
   D. Filing
   E. Using sand paper
   F. Painting
   G. Staining or shellacking

FREE TIME ACTIVITIES

The mentally retarded are apt to find that they have much free time in life. Therefore, they should be given specific training in finding leisure time activities which they can do and which they enjoy. The teacher may assign some of the activities, but she should also encourage the students to choose freely among activities whenever possible.

1. Seatwork assignments
2. Practice files
3. Individual projects
4. Group projects
5. Play materials
6. Peer tutoring
7. Small informal discussions
8. Handicrafts
9. Games
10. Library books
11. Gardening
12. Listening to records
13. Special hobbies

VOCATIONAL TRAINING

1. Knows the roles and responsibilities of persons in various jobs, particularly those jobs which are likely to be available.
2. Knows the qualifications for various available jobs
3. Practices punctuality in arriving to school on time
4. Performs in dramatizations of various work situations
5. Works on group projects with particular responsibilities which are carried on over a period of time (ex. care of school yard for one week, carrying milk to other classrooms)

READING

The educable mentally retarded child should be encouraged to progress as far as he can in reading. However, it must be recognized that he will progress slower than the normal child and he will not reach the expected level of a normal child. Once the educable mentally retarded child has begun reading, many of the normal reading objectives can be employed but presented more slowly and practised more frequently.

However, caution should be used to be sure the child has met all of the readiness objectives before he begins reading.

The mentally retarded child should also be taught a basic sight vocabulary which would include the following types of words: (1) names (ex. streets, city, friends, days of the week, months, school, etc.), (2) safety words (ex. stop, yield, wet floor, danger, poison, etc.), (3) common signs (ex. ladies' room, entrance, bus terms), and (4) food labels. Some trainable mentally retarded children can also be taught this basic sight vocabulary.

I. Prereading readiness skills
 A. Auditory Perception
  1. Can identify and discriminate in his surroundings as to tone
  2. Can listen with attention to rhymes, stories, and songs
  3. Can identify words that rhyme
  4. Can discriminate between beginning sounds and between final sounds
  5. Can hear syllables in spoken words
 B. Visual Perception
  1. Can recognize shapes and pictures
  2. Can recognize differences in shapes and pictures
  3. Can identify and match capital and lower case letters
  4. Can discriminate between letter forms and word forms
 C. Comprehension Development
  1. Call recall events in rhymes, stories, etc.
  2. Can demonstrate his knowledge of a spoken sentence
  3. Demonstrates understanding of words read to him by putting in his own words
  4. Can supply missing words in oral context using word order as a clue to meaning
  5. Can listen to poems and stories and relate the main idea
  6. Associates related ideas
  7. Can arrange pictures to show sequence
  8. Can make inferences from spoken words
  9. Can identify in a spoken sentence the word that does not fit
  10. Can use ideas to make a sentence
  11. Can answer questions
  12. Can draw conclusions
  13. Can associate spoken words with pictures
  14. Can interpret pictures
  15. Can recognize the inflectional endings in spoken words, e.g., -s, -es, -d, -ed, and -ing
 D. Study – Reading
   He can follow simple oral directions
 E. Mechanics of reading
  1. Demonstrates that he understands that numbers, words, and a series of pictures are to be observed from left to right
  2. Understands that the beginning of a printed word is at its left

ARITHMETIC

I. Arithmetic facts and processes

A. Can rote count 1 to 5
B. Can pair objects one to one
C. Can count and display objects 1 to 5
D. Can recognize and form number symbols 1 to 5
E. Can count to 100
F. Can write and use symbols to 20
G. Can tell what number comes before and after
H. Can tell what number is more and less
I. Understands the ordinals first to twentieth
J. Can show addition with objects and by drawing up to 10
K. Can use symbols for single digit addition
L. Can write the number symbols to 100
M. Realizes that many hundreds is more than 1 hundred
N. Can perform the arithmetic processes for addition and subtraction
O. Can use the arithmetic processes to solve problems given in words and in situations
P. Understands 1/2, 1/3, and 1/4

II. Time
A. Knows what a clock is
B. Knows you go to bed at night and get up in the morning
C. Knows lunch is at noon
D. Knows that there are 5 days in a school week and 7 days in a full week
E. Knows the names of the days
F. Can tell time and form time by the hour, the half-hour, and the minute
G. Knows that there are about 30 days in a month
II. Can read a calendar
I. Knows that there are some things that start at a set time (ex. school)

III. Money
A. Can recognize and name the coins
B. Can rename the coins (ex. 5 pennies = 1 nickle)
C. Can use various coins to make different amounts up to $1.00
D. Can make change for up to $1.00
E. Can make purchases for up to $5.00
F. Can read and write money symbols for up to $100.00
G. Knows that a bank is for money transactions

COMMUNICATION SKILLS

I. Comprehension (Receptive Language)
A. Identifies by name familiar objects
B. Understands and will respond to single step commands
C. Understands and will respond to multi-step commands
D. Identifies objects by their use

    E. Can discriminate between adjectives
    F. Can respond to the use of preparations
    G. Likes to hear stories
    H. Follows individual instructions
    I. Follows group instructions

II. Expression (In Sequential Order)
    A. Uses gestures and physical action (ex. grabbing people to get attention, pantomiming)
    B. Tries to use sounds to convey meaning (ex. babbling, using initial sound)
    C. Imitates sounds, words, actions
    D. Attempts to verbalize meaning using single words or combining just 2 or 3 words
    E. Participates in a group, repeating all words, performing before the group
    F. Converses with others
    G. Answers questions
    H. Asks questions
    I. Describes a picture
    J. Can name the colors
    K. Can retell a story
    L. Can pantomime a phrase
    M. Can pantomime a situation
    N. Can ask for directions
    O. Can give directions
    P. Can answer telephone and carry on conversation
    Q. Can take telephone messages
    R. Can make emergency phone call
    S. Accepts and gives criticism on speaking
    T. Speaks in turn
    U. Speaks before peers with ease

III. Writing skills
    A. Holds the writing utensil properly
    B. Can distinguish between the appearances of letters
    C. Can make large muscular movements
    D. Can trace and follow dots
    E. Can put together simple puzzles
    F. Can copy a circle
    G. Can copy a cross
    H. Can copy a square
    I. Can write his name in manuscript
    J. Can copy words
    K. Can copy sentences
    L. Can distinguish between and can form capital and small letters
    M. Begins sentence with capital letter

N. Ends sentence with period or question mark
O. Can write numbers 1 to 100
P. (After understanding the meaning of the parts of a date) can write a date with the month, day, and year such as September 5, 1972
Q. Can write his own street address
R. Can write and address friendly notes including the return address
S. Can write in cursive
T. Can fill in application forms
U. Can use common abbreviations such as Mr., Dr.

HOUSEHOLD ARTS

I. Schoolroom tasks for which students can be responsible
  A. Care of door mat
  B. Clean chalkboard
  C. Sharpen and pass out pencils
  D. Dusting
  E. Care of plants
  F. Care of library table
  G. Care of own desk and locker
  H. Wash windows (on inside)
II. General household skills
  A. Care of floors and woodwork
    1. Cleaning
    2. Waxing
  B. Care of furniture
    1. Dusting
    2. Polishing
  C. Care of kitchen
    1. Care of sink
    2. Care of kitchen utensils
    3. Care and use of small electrical appliances
    4. Care of cupboards
    5. Care of refrigerator
    6. Care of stove
  D. Care of bathroom
    1. Daily care
    2. Weekly care
    3. Cleaning tub and bowls
    4. Changing towels
  E. Care of bedroom
    1. Changing bed linens
    2. Proper storage
  F. Laundering
    1. Using hamper

      2. Sorting clothes

      3. Removing stains

      4. Use and care of machines

      5. Proper washing of various types of clothing

      6. Hanging clothes to dry

      7. Folding and sprinkling clothes

      8. Ironing

III. Safety

    A. Electric plugs

    B. Piled up trash and its dangers

    C. Pot handles

    D. Articles left on stairs

IV. Facts about child care and practice in caring for children

 V. Food

    A. Its preparation

    B. Marketing for food

    C. Planning menus

    D. After meal care

    E. Health and sanitation

VI. Care of clothing

    A. Put away neatly

    B. How to remove spots

    C. How to protect

    D. How to clean and polish shoes and boots

    E. How to sew on buttons

    F. How to mend

SPECIAL CLASSROOM

These are the suggested minimum specifications for a classroom to be used by trainable mentally retarded pupils. Educable mentally retarded children may or may not have a special classroom.

Size: Approximately 24' x 40'

Location: Within easy access to lavatory facilities. However, placement of an atypical class in basement or isolated areas of a school should be avoided.

Appearance: Well-lighted and ventilated, attractively painted.

Furniture: Fifteen movable, noiseless desks and chairs of sizes suitable for children who will use the room.
File cabinet with lock.
Teacher's desk and chair.
Bookcases.
Library table — round or rectangular, with chairs.
Work table.
Equipped woodworking bench.
Paint table with metal top.
Sewing machine with equipment.
Phonograph or piano.
Cabinets for storage of paints, tools, supplies.
Bins for display and storage of pupils' handwork, finished and unfinished.
Easels.
Lumber rack.

Facilities: Sink with hot and cold water.
Stove with oven.
Refrigerator.
At least three electrical outlets.
Chalkboard and bulletin boards.
Adequate space apart from classroom proper for teacher's and children's coats, hats, and rainwear.

Supplies: Similar to those given to regular classrooms with these additions:

Sewing materials.
Woodworking tools and supplies.
Weaving materials.
Cooking utensils and supplies.
Additional handicraft tools and equipment according to pupils' abilities and needs.
(Appendix C has suggestions for special class equipment and supplies.)

PROPOSED CLASSROOM FOR MENTALLY RETARDED PUPILS

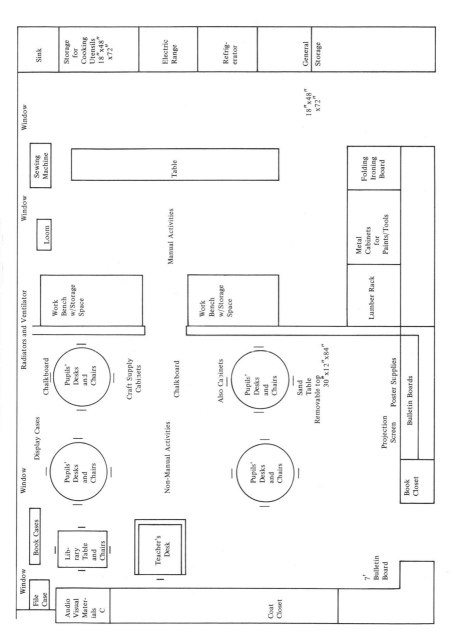

APPENDIX C

USEFUL CLASSROOM FURNISHINGS, EQUIPMENT AND SUPPLIES

Abacus
Aquarium
Art supplies
Athletic equipment including
  Balls (all sizes)
  Bats
  Mats, tumbling
  Ropes, jumping
Bins, storage
Blocks, work and number building
Board, magnetic or flannel
Board, peg
Board, stencil
Boards, bulletin or tack
Bookcases
Books, low reading level, high interest level
Cabinet, filing w/lock
Cabinet, first aid
Cabinets, general storage
Cages, small wire, animal
Camera
Cases, display w/shelves
Chalkboards
Clay, modeling
Clock dial
Closets, storage
Counting boxes with numerals and objects
Craft-supplies
Cubes, color
Desks and chairs, movable and adjustable (pupils' and teacher's)
Devices, arithmetic drill
Discs, counting
Dominoes
Duplicator, fluid-type machine
Easels

Games, remedial reading
Health materials
  Toothbrushes
  Combs
  Nail clippers
  Nail files
  Soap
Instruments, musical for rhythm work
Kiln
Lockers, pupil
Letters, cut-out
Looms
Machine, mimeograph
Machines, remedial reading
Maps, wall
Money, toy
Napkins, paper
Pictures, suitable
Poster supplies
Projector, filmstrip
Projector, sound film
Puzzles
Racks, wire
Radio
Record player
Register, toy cash
Rulers
Science kit
Screen, projection
Screens, folding
Set, alphabet
Shelves, exhibit
Stopwatch
Store, play w/play money
Straws, paper
Table, library, w/chairs
Table, sand (removable top)

Addenda*

Aprons
Barber kit
Basin w/hot and cold water
Bed, small, single w/linens
Benches, work
Board, bread
Board, folding ironing
Bowls, mixing
Cabinets, tool
Chair, barber's
Cleansers, soap
Combs, barber
Cupboards
Cups, measuring
Cutlery
Dishcloths
Dishes
Dishtowels
Dressings, hair
Dressmaking equipment
First aid equipment
Forks
Iron, electric
Kettle, soup
Knives
Machines, clothes washing

Machines, sewing
Mirror
Pans
Powder, soap
Rack, lumber
Refrigerator, automatic
Removers, spot
Scales, produce
Sheets, cookie
Sink w/hot and cold water
Spoons
Sterilizer
Straws, wooden
Stove w/oven or hot plate, two-burner
Tablecloth, oilcloth
Tables, work
Tailoring supplies
Tape measure
Tape recorder
Television set
Terrarium
Towels, paper
Toys, music (Tonettes, Humazoos, etc.)
Typewriters
Utensils, cooking

*During the time that the mentally retarded child is in school, these major areas of experience can be taught: THE HOME, THE NEIGHBORHOOD, THE CITY, and OCCUPATIONS. Since these children usually leave school at a relatively early age, emphasis should be placed on career education: finding and getting a job, spending one's income, and being a good worker as a citizen and social being. Emphasis may also be placed on the nonmanual or social skills since mentally retarded children will seldom exceed a third or fourth grade level in most academic skills. Nonmanual or social skills may include personal health and appearance; manners; means of getting employment; means of keeping a job; means of adjusting to accidents and unemployment; ways to get along with the "boss"; ways to get along with fellow workers; budget and banking; ways to travel in the city; suggestions for living at home; suggestions for living away from home; recreation; personal relationships; and citizenship.

The classroom furnishings, equipment, and supplies that have been listed can enable the teacher and teacher aide to provide a functional and realistic curriculum for their pupils.

APPENDIX D

PROPOSED REPORT CARD

REPORT TO PARENTS

19___ – 19___

PUPIL'S NAME: _____

PLACEMENT: _____

SCHOOL: _____

ADDRESS: _____

TEACHERS: _____

To Parents and Guardians:

Please read this report carefully to understand the progress of your child. It will show you how the teacher is helping him to become a good worker and citizen.

The school wishes to work in close cooperation with the home to promote the growth of effective citizenship.

Conferences with the teacher will help both parent and teacher to plan your child's continued development. Such conferences should be arranged with the teacher in advance.

SUGGESTED DATE AND TIME FOR CONFERENCES:

Report 1. _____
Report 2. _____
Report 3. _____
Report 4. _____

V. EFFORT AND GENERAL CONDUCT:

Report 1. _____

Report 2. _____

Report 3. _____

Report 4. _____

*General Rating: S – Pupil is making satisfactory progress consistent with his ability to learn. U–Pupil's progress is unsatisfactory and is not equal to his ability to learn.

ATTENDANCE:

Report	1	2	3	4
DAYS ABSENT				
NO. TIMES TARDY				
PLACEMENT IN SEPTEMBER				

PARENT'S REPLY AND COMMENTS:
(Attach additional sheet if necessary.)

Report 1. _____ Signature: _____

Report 2. _____ Signature: _____

Report 3. _____ Signature: _____

Report 4. _____ Signature: _____

Reverse Side of Report Card for Mentally Retarded Pupils

REPORT TO PARENTS

PUPIL'S NAME:_____ General Ratings*

DATES: 1._____ 3._____ Report 1 2 3 4

2._____ 4._____ [ ] [ ] [ ] [ ]

I. OUTSTANDING FEATURES OF PUPIL'S WORK:

Report 1._____

Report 2._____

Report 3._____

Report 4._____

II. PHASES OF THE SCHOOL PROGRAM IN WHICH HE IS MAKING SATISFACTORY PROGRESS:

Report 1._____

Report 2._____

Report 3._____

Report 4._____

III. PHASES OF THE SCHOOL PROGRAM IN WHICH HE NEEDS SPECIAL HELP AND CAN MAKE IMPROVEMENT:

Report 1._____

Report 2._____

Report 3._____

Report 4._____

IV. HEALTH:

Report 1._____

Report 2._____

Report 3._____

Report 4._____

APPENDIX E

SUPPLEMENTARY RECORD

Growth of Child

Date

ATTITUDES AND HABITS	STRENGTH	WEAKNESS
1. Is able to work and play with others	————	————
2. Is able to play and work safely	————	————
3. Is punctual — coming to school from recess period — going home	————	————
4. Is courteous and respects the rights of others	————	————
5. Is able to finish a task	————	————
6. Is beginning to work independently	————	————
7. Puts forth best effort	————	————

ACADEMIC SKILLS

1. Reading level (circle one)

   Readiness   Pre-Primer   First Reader   Other

   List book or books child is able to read and understand:
   1.
   2.

2. ARITHMETIC LEVEL (circle one)

   Readiness   First Grade   Second Grade   Other

	STRENGTH	WEAKNESS
Understands number meanings	————	————
Is able to handle basic combinations and separations	————	————
Understands money — for buying crackers in school going to the store	———— ————	———— ————

3. HANDWRITING

	STRENGTH	WEAKNESS
Is learning to write legibly	————	————
Name	————	————
Address	————	————
Short sentences	————	————

136

STRENGTH   WEAKNESS

4. Social Studies (List Social Studies units experienced this year on other side of page.)

Is learning to contribute to the group   _____ _____
Is learning to listen to others   _____ _____

CASCADE SYSTEM OF SPECIAL EDUCATION SERVICE

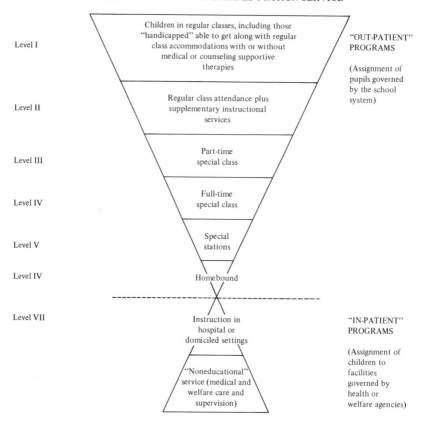

Level I — Children in regular classes, including those "handicapped" able to get along with regular class accommodations with or without medical or counseling supportive therapies

Level II — Regular class attendance plus supplementary instructional services

Level III — Part-time special class

Level IV — Full-time special class

Level V — Special stations

Level IV — Homebound

Level VII — Instruction in hospital or domiciled settings

"Noneducational" service (medical and welfare care and supervision)

"OUT-PATIENT" PROGRAMS

(Assignment of pupils governed by the school system)

"IN-PATIENT" PROGRAMS

(Assignment of children to facilities governed by health or welfare agencies)

Figure 2. The cascade system of special education service. The tapered design indicates the considerable difference in the numbers involved at the different levels and calls attention to the fact that the system serves as a diagnostic filter. The most specialized facilities are likely to be needed by the fewest children on a long term basis. This organizational model can be applied to development of special education services for all types of disability.

— Evelyn Deno. "Special Education as Developmental Capitol," *Exceptional Children,* 37:229-237, November, 1970.

PARENT CHECKLIST

Child's Name: _____   Date: _____

Circle the number which describes your child (as closely as possible). If the statement *rarely* describes him, circle (1) after the statement, if it *sometimes* describes him circle (2), if it *always* describes him circle (3). Follow this procedure for each statement.

	Rarely	*Sometimes*	*Always*
1. Can kick a ball six feet _____	1	2	3
2. Stands up straight with good posture___	1	2	3
3. Listens to records and tries to sing with them _____	1	2	3
4. Dresses and undresses himself with your help _____	1	2	3
5. Ties his own shoes _____	1	2	3
6. Polishes his own shoes_____	1	2	3
7. Washes his hands and face unassisted___	1	2	3
8. Applies his own toothpaste and brushes his teeth _____	1	2	3
9. Cleans his own nose if it is running_____	1	2	3
10. Can cut food with a knife unassisted___	1	2	3
11. Can use a fork properly when eating___	1	2	3
12. Helps prepare sandwiches_____	1	2	3
13. Can make jello or pudding_____	1	2	3
14. Helps set the table by placing things where you tell him_____	1	2	3
15. Sets the table with utensils in proper place unassisted_____	1	2	3
16. Helps clear the table without breaking dishes _____	1	2	3
17. Takes initiative in cleaning up his own mess _____	1	2	3
18. Reports accidents (spilling, etc.)_____	1	2	3
19. Completes task after being asked, such as cleaning own room_____	1	2	3
20. Can pay attention to a task for ten minutes _____	1	2	3
21. Makes own bed_____	1	2	3

	Rarely	Sometimes	Always
22. Sweeps floor and pushes dirt in dust pan	1	2	3
23. Gets in and out of car unassisted_____.	1	2	3
24. Does not lose his balance easily_____.	1	2	3
25. Can stay on a line when cutting with scissors ----------------------.	1	2	3
26. Runs without falling _____	1	2	3
27. Can stay within the lines when cutting with scissors---------------------	1	2	3
28. Can catch a large play ball which you have thrown to him_____	1	2	3
29. Can skip_____	1	2	3
30. Can jump on both feet._____	1	2	3
31. Can hop on one foot _____	1	2	3
32. Can touch his toes when bending at the waist (knees unbent) _____	1	2	3
33. Can climb steps adult-fashion by placing one foot on each succeeding step_____·	1	2	3
34. Respond correctly to words such as in front of, behind, on and off _____	1	2	3
35. Can be sent on errands with note_____·	1	2	3
36. Can answer the telephone and take messages -----------------------	1	2	3
37. Shares toys with others_____·	1	2	3
38. Plays with others -----------------	1	2	3
39. Offers to help other children or adults	1	2	3
40. Can speak in complete sentences ----·	1	2	3
41. When speaking, can be understood by most persons-------------------	1	2	3
42. Can state full name _____	1	2	3
43. Follows directions the first time you tell him -------------------------	1	2	3
44. Can name objects in pictures and story books--------------------------	1	2	3
45. Can name or identify the colors — red, green, blue, yellow----------------	1	2	3
46. Can imitate an action you tell him to do	1	2	3
47. Can listen to a record and do what the voice tells him to do _____.	1	2	3
48. Likes to do exercises and play active games -----------------------·	1	2	3
49. Has confidence in himself-----------	1	2	3

APPENDIX H

CHILD DEVELOPMENT SCALE

Board of Education of the City of New York
Bureau of Education Research
YORK CHILD DEVELOPMENT SCALES
Ages 4 through 7

Scale A Scale B Scale L S.P.

Score _____

Date of Rating _____

Age at Rating _____

Rating _____

Boy_____ Girl _____

Date of Birth _____

School:_____ Borough _____Class ___

Teacher _____

1. Markedly
   Above Average _____
2. Above Average _____
3. Average _____
4. Below Average _____
5. Markedly
   Below Average _____

SCALE A: PERSONAL INDEPENDENCE

Age Level Three

_____1. Unbottons and takes off coat and jacket without assistance.

_____2. Goes to toilet himself; may need some help with clothing.

_____3. Gives his full name.

_____4. Helps put toys away, perhaps only as game with adult.

_____5. Occupies himself with toys in playground or yard without constant supervision.

Age Level Four

_____6. Puts on coat and buttons it without assistance.

_____7. Takes care of toilet needs independently.

_____8. Replaces toys and work materials, does simple routine housekeeping tasks in classroom; may need constant encouragement and frequent reminders.

_____9. Evaluates his behavior; probably praises himself and his products uncritically.

_____10. Shows judgement of difficulty of various activities; generally undertakes those within his ability, although he may need some help.

Age Level Five

_____11. Accepts responsibility for cleaning work place, and for replacing materials; may need encouragement.

_____12. Assumes responsibility for bringing money for purchasing milk, crackers, etc.

_____13. Begins to show discrimination in evaluating his performance; wants product to conform to original idea and to function crudely.

_____14. Wants to finish what he has started, if the work is interesting and within his ability, even if it takes several days.

_____15. Gives his home address.

Age Level Six

_____16. Is independent in dressing, including putting on rubbers.

_____17. Can go to school without an adult if there are no dangerous crossings.

_____18. Carries out class routines like distributing work materials, milk, etc.

_____19. Works independently for half hour or more on block construction, painting, etc., if given free choice of familiar activities.

_____20. Finds in the classroom or at home pictures appropriate to the class topic of study; this is done voluntarily or by assignment.

Age Level Seven

_____21. Shifts from one job to another according to plan without reminder.

_____22. Begins to judge products as to levels of skill and craftsmanship.

_____23. Begins simple concrete planning with a group under adult guidance.

_____24. Refers to books and magazines in the class collection to find very simple information, using both pictures and text.

_____25. Finds rooms anywhere in building if numbers are given.

Age Level Eight

_____26. Tells time correctly, at least to the nearest quarter hour.

_____27. Under adult guidance, does his part in managing and in keeping simple records for a routine class or school job, such as ordering and distributing milk.

_____28. Under adult guidance, plans and carries out a sequence of steps in a project.

_____29. Obtains information on class topic of interest from a variety of sources; e.g., books, people, souvenirs, libraries, museums, etc.

_____30. Uses writing independently, as in short notes or letters.

SCALE B: INTERPERSONAL RELATIONS

Age Level Three

_____1. Has attained consciousness of self; thinks and talks mostly in terms of I or me.

_____2. Begins to play with, rather than alongside of another child.

_____3. Begins to take turns if waiting period is short, but may frequently hit, grab, push to get what he wants.

_____4. With adult guidance, begins to share, but may frequently cry, hit, have temper tantrums when deprived of what he wants.

_____5. Takes role of animals or people in dramatic play.

Age Level Four

_____ 6. Plays cooperatively with another child; there is definite although not necessarily continuous interaction between them.

_____ 7. Seeks status in group; may do this by giving outstanding performance or by bragging or showing off.

_____ 8. Uses spoken requests to get what he wants, although hitting and snatching may still be frequent.

_____ 9. Generally accepts an alternative for something he wants and cannot have.

_____10. Suggests taking turns, although may not carry through the process consistently.

Age Level Five

_____11. Plays cooperatively with a group of two to five children; interaction is not necessarily continuous.

_____12. Sustains for long period interest in dramatic play with others.

_____13. Comforts other children when they cry or have been hurt.

_____14. Shares tools and equipment voluntarily with others within organized work group.

_____15. Expresses anger; form of expression begins to be verbal rather than physical.

Age Level Six

_____16. Plays group games with simple structure and rules, as in tag, jump rope.

_____17. Expresses anger, usually in words rather than physically.

_____18. Takes initiative in helping younger or less able children in classroom routines.

_____19. Re-enacts in detail the functions of neighborhood workers — the policeman, garbageman, grocer, laundryman, etc.

_____20. Notices and makes comments about the contributions and productions of other children.

Age Level Seven

_____21. Shows loyalty to a small group of children; chooses its members for voluntary group activities.

_____22. Adheres strictly to group-made rules to conduct for games or classroom activities; will not tolerate exceptions.

_____23. Evaluates criticisms by other children and accepts constructive suggestions.

_____24. Expresses common adult opinions about personalities in the news.

_____25. Re-enacts role of adult hero or heroine in narrative sequences drawn from stories or motion pictures.

Age level Eight

_____26. Participates in group games with definite rules and rather involved relationships as in baseball, punchball, or as in table games like parchesi, pick-up-sticks.

_____27. Understands need for the simpler social courtesies and generally uses them without teacher reminder.

_____28. Begins to consider approval and opinions of other children of major importance in guiding behavior.

_____29. Shows social consciousness in seeing similarities between himself and child of different background.

_____30. Judges critically the capabilities of other children in selecting them for special jobs.

SCALE L: LANGUAGE

Age Level Three

_____1. Articulates in understandable but infantile manner.

_____2. Begins to talk in short sentences (three or four words); grammatical structure may be poor.

_____3. Keeps up a continuous monologue regarding the things he sees and does.

_____4. Asks *What's that? What's your name?* repeats answer until he has added new word to his vocabulary.

_____5. Relates incidents in simple terms with few details.

Age Level Four

_____6. Uses sentences averaging five or six words; grammatical structure may be poor.

_____7. Plays with sounds; makes up nonsense words and rhymed syllables.

_____8. Uses numbers without necessarily understanding their meaning.

_____9. Asks *How?* and *Why?* repeatedly, more to establish relationship with the adult than to obtain information.

_____10. Talks to other children; probably not expect a reply.

Age Level Five

_____11. Articulates clearly all sounds; possible exceptions *th, zh, wh,* triple consonants like *str, sts.*

_____12. Reports in some detail events recently experienced or witnessed.

_____13. Adapts his language to role of mother, father, etc. in dramatic play.

_____14. Recognizes and gives correct name for common colors.

_____15. Asks questions for the definite purpose of obtaining information.

Age Level Six

_____16. Uses fairly accurate grammatical forms.

____17. Uses some compound and some complex sentences.

____18. Uses polysyllabic words such as *elevator, apologize.*

____19. Retells a complete story like *The Three Little Pigs* or *Goldilocks* with events in sequence.

____20. Adjusts his language to fit roles of storybook characters in unrehearsed dramatizations.

Age Level Seven

____21. Has mastered the mechanics of articulation.

____22. Uses sentences with grammatical structure roughly approximating that of the adult; uses all parts of speech.

____23. Contributes to interchange of ideas in sustained conversation.

____24. Is aware of humorous possibilities and double meanings of words; enjoys puns.

____25. Uses idiomatic expressions such as *raining cats and dogs, get a wiggle on, clear as mud.*

Age Level Eight

____26. Uses some current slang, technical or specialized terms.

____27. Gives meanings of words in descriptive terms.

____28. Participates in discussion and defends his point of view.

____29. Shows beginning appreciation of abstract ideas in conversation.

____30. Sees new interpretations or several meanings in familiar words.

SOCIAL DEVELOPMENT

(By Teacher)

	YES	NO	
1. Asks to go to toilet.	____	____	1.
2. Initiates own play activities.	____	____	2.
3. Removes coat or dress.	____	____	3.
4. Eats with fork.	____	____	4.
5. Gets drink unassisted.	____	____	5.
6. Dries own hands	____	____	6.
7. Avoids simple hazards.	____	____	7.
8. Puts on coat or dress unassisted.	____	____	8.
9. Cuts with scissors.	____	____	9.
10. Relates experiences.	____	____	10.
11. Walks down stairs one step per tread.	____	____	11.
12. Plays cooperatively at kindergarten level.	____	____	12.
13. Buttons coat or dress.	____	____	13.
14. Helps at little household tasks.	____	____	14.
15. "Performs" for others.	____	____	15.

	YES	NO	
16. Washes hands unaided.	____	____	16.
17. Cares for self at toilet.	____	____	17.
18. Washes face unassisted.	____	____	18.
19. Goes about neighborhood unattended.	____	____	19.
20. Dresses self except tying.	____	____	20.
21. Uses pencil or crayon for drawing.	____	____	21.
22. Plays competitive exercise games.	____	____	22.
23. Prints simple words.	____	____	23.
24. Uses skates, sled, wagon.	____	____	24.
25. Plays simple table games.	____	____	25.
26. Is trusted with money.	____	____	26.
27. Goes to school unattended.	____	____	27.
28. Uses table knife for spreading.	____	____	28
29. Uses pencil for writing.	____	____	29.
30. Bathes self assisted.	____	____	30.
31. Goes to bed unassisted.	____	____	31.
32. Tells time to quarter hour.	____	____	32.
33. Uses table knife for cutting.	____	____	33.
34. Disavows literal Santa Claus.	____	____	34.
35. Participates in preadolescent play.	____	____	35.
36. Combs or brushes hair.	____	____	36.

NAME INDEX

147

SUBJECT INDEX

A

AAMD definition of retarded, 11
  debate regarding, 12
Abilities of child,
  assessment essential, 57
  parents' checklist, 139-140
Academic achievement,
  emphasis not desirable, 56
  inappropriate for grading retardate,
    42, 60
Achievement of pupil, evaluation, 50-62,
  107
  importance, 75
Activities of school personnel, coordination, 76-79
Adaptive behavior, impairment evidences, 11-12
Adjustment,
  present and future, program to de-
    velop, 23
  social factors, 96
Administrators,
  assessment of pupils, 48
  assessment of retardates' progress, 57,
    60, 61
  flexibility needed, 109
  goal setting, 52
  guidance role, 19
  placement decisions, 33
  preparation needs, 38
  responsibilities, 15-16, 26
  role in
    grouping, 21
    innovations, 44
    placement of pupils, 103
    total approach, 48
  special requirements, 108
  training needed, 44
Age levels,
  interpersonal relations, 142-144

language abilities, 144-145
personal independence evidences,
  141-142
social development, 145-146
Aim, education of retarded, 102
American Association on Mental Deficiency, see AAMD
Anecdotal records, achievement evaluation aid, 50
Arithmetic, abilities, 124-125
Art, projects, 121
Assessment,
  continuous, program development aid,
    42-43
  desired goals, 34
Assessment of needs, steps required,
  40-42
Attention span, limited in retardates, 53
Audio-visual aids, program assessment
  use, 41

B

Basic Guides, see Guides
Behavior,
  achievement evaluation aid, 51
  directing to desirable ends, 20
Bibliographies, 113-116
Binet-Simon intelligence test, 5
Blind, 4
  see also Visual defects

C

California, speech studies, 68
Cascade system, special education, 138
  fig.
Categorizing practices, criticism of, 21
Certification requirements, principals, 26
  see also Principals
Child,

149